endorsements

"Accessible without losing its edge, the language fantastically compelling while also being as precise and uncompromising as a bullet."

> —**Benjanun Sriduangkaew**, award-nominated author of *Scale-Bright*, the upcoming *Winterglass*, and various stories appearing in *Clarkesworld*, *Apex*, and collections of the year's best speculative fiction.

"This book is an unapologetic, militant critique of contemporary capitalism. Moufawad-Paul's skillful arguments are a testament to the necessary centrality of class politics, indeed class war, to any anti-capitalist struggle worthy of its name. Drawing not only on Marx, Lenin, and Mao, but also more recent analyses, this book disassembles the politics of austerity in our world, offering hope that the left can be, or is, more than the sum of its parts."

> —**Colleen Bell**, Assistant Professor of Political Studies at University of Saskatchewan, author of *The Freedom of Security* and co-editor of *War, Police, and Assemblages of Intervention*.

Austerity Apparatus
by J. Moufawad-Paul

ISBN 978-1-894946-89-6

Copyright 2017 J. Moufawad-Paul
This edition copyright 2017 Kersplebedeb
First printing

Kersplebedeb Publishing and Distribution
CP 63560 | CCCP Van Horne | Montreal, Quebec | H3W 3H8

email: info@kersplebedeb.com
web: www.kersplebedeb.com
           www.leftwingbooks.net

Copies available from AK Press:

AK Press | 370 Ryan Ave. #100 | Chico, CA | 95973

phone: (510) 208–1700
email: info@akpress.org
web: akpress.org

Printed in Canada

AUSTERITY APPARATUS

J. Moufawad-Paul

This one is for Vicky

"...assemblages allow for complicities of privilege and the production of new normativities even as they cannot anticipate spaces and moments of resistance..."

Jasbir Puar, *Terrorist Assemblages*

"I call 'communism' the real movement that elaborates, everywhere and at every moment, civil war."

Tiqqun, *Introduction to Civil War*

foreword

What a mistake it was to recognize *austerity*. In 2009 a British conservative, avatar of the old empire, declared an "Age of Austerity" as fact. Before long, the term achieved conceptual status, a maggot deposited in the ear of everyone who bothered to listen, or listened to those who listened. A brain worm producing lesions on the mind of the mainstream left in the imperialist metropoles.

Before 2009 we rarely used the word *austerity*. Conservative economists and IMF apparatchiks would speak of "austerity measures" (the concept was not conjured from nothing) but the establishment of an "Age of Austerity" turned the word into a popular discourse that demanded respect. For that which is austere ought to command our attention; that which is true is also strict, cold, factual—like a simple algebraic operation where 2 is forced by $1+1$.

The word-become-concept proliferates, demanding recognition. It is no longer just a word coined by conservative politicians, or even an economic concept spouted by the organic intellectuals of the imperial-capitalist order as it was before; it has become an ideological state apparatus, the austerity apparatus. It produces subject positions just as it produces its own conceptual development. Its "age" is a myth insofar as it was established by a reactionary politician who would have endorsed the same policies, in any period, regardless of how he chose to semantically codify those policies. It is a concrete fact insofar as it has become a theoretical concept, the buzz-word that mediates a multitude of crisis capitalist policies.

Before the austerity apparatus we spoke of neoliberal capitalism and the multiple policies it enacted during its crises, none of which were new, but we never tired of developing new words for old trends—"casualization," "precarity," and others. These terms, and others like them, can now be understood as part of a singular apparatus which is in fact a modern rearticulation of an atavistic norm: the production of surplus-value, the extraction of surplus-labour.

As the cliché goes, the more things change the more they stay the same. Not a very progressive cliché: a truism for conservatives about a static world; a claim that there is no such thing as change when change is a fact of history and biology; a demand that things ought to stay the same because that is just how reality is even though this *is* is taken for granted. Then again, the discursive universe governed by the austerity apparatus would like us to believe that change is impossible, that austerity is both new and the limit of the real.

Under capitalism, then, things change while staying the same. A mutation of the interior takes place, a transformation and rebranding of older trends, to mirror the formal changes of the social formation. They weren't using computers in 19th century work houses, were they? No, but they were producing surplus-value and extracting surplus-labour and that, more than the development of new machinery, is what matters.

Capitalism is adept at changing everything while changing nothing. *Everything* on the level of appearance, the in/formal operations. *Nothing* on the level of substance—such a transformation would require the end of capitalism as capitalism.

Hence, a year before this apparatus had a name, right at the moment when it was being generated as an apparatus, those of us involved in labour disruptions at the heart of the imperialist metropoles were already primed for its discourse. In 2008 we were told that it was "not the time" for strikes since workers needed to "tighten their belts" in these "tough times." That there was "not enough money to go around" and that even the blandest economistic struggles were selfish. By 2009, every anti-worker ideologue and their devotees had a popularized concept under which to mobilize their arguments about how and why workers should absorb the excesses of those capitalists who wanted to maintain their wealthy lifestyles: austerity. In this sense, the austerity apparatus is simply that which functions to police the everyday operations of crisis capitalism. In another sense this apparatus is the mobilization of operations that are a normative part of capitalism *even without a crisis.* But this is simply due to the fact that economic crises are also part of capitalism's day-to-day functioning: capitalism is crisis, implicitly or explicitly.

Here we have three regulative functions of the capitalist state of affairs: a state of social peace, sometimes called the welfare state; a state of anxiety, sometimes called neoliberalism; a state of emergency, sometimes called fascism. Today's austerity apparatus emerges in a state of anxiety, promising a state of emergency while mobilizing its discontents to focus only on a return to a state of social peace rather than challenge the state of affairs as a whole. The class struggle—the civil war that lurks at the heart of every state—is thus contained.

Before 2009 the austerity apparatus was still

being built, now it is ascendant. A novel re-presentation of the old, a different composition of the same, it attempts to prolong business as usual while simultaneously proclaiming its uniqueness.

on the management of civil war; austerity as collaboration

"The political imaginary of class warfare has its own horrors. Because class war is civil war, the war zone is superimposed upon the space of the 'normal' state, so that, potentially, all of civil society is under siege."

Susan Buck-Morss, *Dreamworld and Catastrophe*

1 Austerity has become that which must be defeated at any cost to the extent that the strategy intended to challenge austerity has now become a strategy that also preserves its basis. Austerity is thus a cunning machine developed by crisis capitalism to channel dissent into the protection of capital itself. The strength of this apparatus is not that it conceals the ravages of capitalism from the masses, but that it proclaims them openly so that austerity and not capitalism will be challenged.

The material basis of the misery exacerbated by brutal austerity policies and practices is not "austerity" anymore than the misery of a cancer patient is located in abnormal bleeding, cysts, and infections. These symptoms are indeed brutal, but if the physician mistakes them as the disease then the patient will have little hope of surviving. And if it suddenly became a medical practice to ignore the cancer and focus only on the symptoms we would be correct to conclude that these doctors were collaborating with cancer.

Hence, that which has branded itself *austerity* is nothing more than the conventionalization of symptoms all of which are dependent on capitalism itself, particularly crisis capitalism. The conventions are clear: cut social services, gut welfare capitalism, reproletarianize the more privileged ranks of the working class, sink the ravages of contemporary capitalism in the global peripheries, and make the poorest workers and non-workers pay with their bodies and lives. All in the interest of allowing the ruling class to persist in generating enough surplus-value for the cancer stage of capitalism so that, by surviving as a class, capitalism can also persist.

The conventions become an apparatus—*the austerity apparatus*—that keeps the patient of the social body breathing. A rather useful apparatus in a world where technicians, rather than physicians, reign supreme: a world in which partial knowledge is celebrated, where a "totalizing" analysis is treated with disdain, and where long term restorative care is ignored in the interest of immediate damage control. You enter that room with the patient and think only of the problems of the life support system—how it can be jerry-rigged, how its tubes and wires can be fixed—than the disease that devours the body. You fix the machine and you succeed in marginally extending the life of the terminal patient, refusing to recognize that all you have done is ensure that their symptoms will eventually become worse, that the next apparatus will be less effective and perhaps more brutal.

In this sense, the austerity apparatus generates collaboration.

2 The austerity apparatus normalizes crisis capitalism. By functioning so as to draw attention to itself as a social fact it obscures the logic of its construction, or at the very least distracts us from focusing on this logic. The austerity apparatus proclaims its existence as a fact, more real than that which generates its facticity, and demands collaboration: austerity is here, it is a reality that cannot be denied, focus on this and only this! Even if we believe ourselves canny enough to see through its deceit and are able to openly proclaim why and how this apparatus came into existence, our attention is still often caught within the workings of the apparatus itself, our strategy limited by its operations.

How else can we explain the excitement amongst the left that was caused by Syriza's 2015 victory in Greece? The excited were also those who simultaneously admitted that Syriza's anti-austerity program was not tantamount to a total, anti-capitalist program. They were still distracted, despite their claims that they were not, to the point that they demanded similar experiments *even in the midst of Syriza's absorption* by the austerity apparatus. And when the absorption was complete—when Syriza capitulated as we should have known it would—the excited either feigned shock or argued that capitulation was the only revolutionary option. Hence:

A reformist discourse dominates the movement, most notably articulated by the trade union, student, and community apparatuses. This discourse instrumentally mobilizes the just demands of the people with its misleading diagnosis of the current social and political situation as one of simple mismanagement of the state by the current regime under the influence of greed and neoliberal ideology. [...] The struggle to satisfy the people's needs is routed onto the dead end and illusory path of redeveloping the management of public finances and taxation. [...] The above strategy is doomed to fail. To correctly diagnose the problem is to admit that austerity is primarily the inevitable consequence of the deep crisis of capitalism. The 2008 financial crash and the following worldwide recession is a brutal reminder of this historical reality: the bourgeoisie, collapsing under the over-accumulation of capital, is finding it more difficult to extract the profits from production. Its only options are on the one hand, to throw itself into financial speculation—until the outbreak of the next bubble and the evaporation of its fictitious wealth—and in other hand, to wage a ruthless struggle against the proletariat by increasing exploitation to extract more value. The policies of austerity are a necessary condition for this second objective. They now represent the ultimate horizon of capitalism.[1]

And yet we need to go even further: a correct diagnosis is not only admitting that austerity is the result of "the deep crisis of capitalism"—even many of those drawn to a reformist strategy might admit this, in word if not in deed—but in recognizing that this deep crisis, this "ultimate horizon," has been part of everyday capitalism since its inception.

3 The discourse of austerity is essential to the austerity apparatus. This discourse is more than reformist, though it does function to mobilize reformism as the only "reasonable" response to its discursive hegemony, but concerns the epistemological status of austerity itself. We are meant to believe that austerity policies are a new development, an emergency that requires the entirety of our focus. But capitalism has always desired this austerity and has, for the most part, successfully functioned as completely austere. The "kinder, gentler" capitalism challenged by austerity (i.e. welfare capitalism) only came into being because of struggles against an older norm that resembled what we would now classify as "austerity measures." In his analysis of how a regulated working-day came to be, Marx sketched out the way in which capitalism typically functioned to promote "Houses of Terror" where workers would be worked as long as possible and under the most brutal methods, since a reserve army meant that they existed in large supply. He concluded:

> Capital cares nothing for the length of life of labour-power. All that concerns it is simply and solely the maximum of labour-power, that can be rendered fluent in a working-day. It attains this end by shortening the extent of the labourer's life, as a

greedy farmer snatches increased produce from the soil by robbing it of its fertility. [...] The capitalistic mode of production... produces thus, with the extension of the working-day, not only the deterioration of human labour-power by robbing it of its normal, moral and physical, conditions of development and function. It produces also the premature exhaustion and death of this labour-power itself.[2]

Thus, "the passion of capital for an unlimited and reckless extension" of exploitation—of what now is rebaptized as *austerity*—is always mediated by limits imposed by "a protracted civil war, more or less dissembled, between the capitalist class and the working-class."[3]

More importantly, however, this kind of *austere* capitalism remains the norm for the majority of the world. Billions of workers labour according to the work-house ethos of 18th and 19th century capitalism described in Marx's *Capital* or Engels's *The Condition of the Working Class in England*, meaning that this is also the ethos of 20th and 21st century capitalism, at least for most of the world's working population. To think of it as *austere*—as if capitalists have suddenly become more vicious than they already were—is to become enraptured by the discursive myth of the austerity apparatus.

This myth is necessary for the daily functioning

of the austerity apparatus: it makes the myth of a reformed capitalism palatable, prevents recognition of proletarianization, and permits us to ignore the fact that our "kinder, gentler" capitalism is just as *austere*. Just as the ruling class demands that the working poor of the imperialist metropoles absorb the excesses of the crisis so that the capitalists can continue to extort the same level of surplus-value, during times of imperialist stability the working class of the same metropoles will not cease to insist, though not always explicitly, that the workers of the so-called "third world" absorb the excesses of global capitalism so that imperial citizens can enjoy the limited benefits of social democracy.

4 Although what is now called "austerity" is capitalism's "ultimate horizon" (and communism its altimate horizon), it would be a mistake to believe that this horizon is reached by an acceleration of its contradictions. Barring limits imposed by proletarian struggle, this vicious tendency is the normal speed of capitalism: to work to death every labourer and devour the entirety of the natural world in the process. This is indeed business as usual for most peoples and regions in the world. And yet, at the imperial metropoles, there has been a resurgence of the theory of "accelerationism" that is proffered as a response to this age of austerity.

Accelerationism is a position that accepts the discourse of the austerity apparatus.

5 The "post-capitalist" variant of acceleration-ism assumes that the contradictions of capitalism, already increasing in velocity in the age of austerity, need to be accelerated further so as to cause the mode of production to collapse under the weight of its unsustainable logic. Rather than investing in resistant movements, the argument goes, we should instead promote this acceleration so that the technologies and processes that capitalism cannot contain will produce a post-capitalist world. This theory is rather old: it was the basis of Fabian socialism in the 19th Century; it was the logic behind the "productive forces" theory of the mid-20th Century. The logic is quite asinine in its assumption that technologies mobilized by capitalism will necessarily lead to capitalism's end. Revolutionary agency is not required, or at the very least is just pulled along by forces of production that function as laws of nature, and only the objective dimension of history (a history of things and artifacts) rather than the subjective dimension (a history of masses, social movements, classes) matters.

Marx and Engels branded this analysis *utopian* because, among other things, it refused to grasp the basis of the objective motion of history—the fact that productive forces are always mediated by productive relations, that value is determined by humans labouring in a particular moment according to particular class relations—and assumed that a socialist order was predestined by capitalism's machines. Walter Benjamin, in *Theses on the Philosophy of History*, attacked the same analysis of capitalism when he accused the German Social Democrats of the Second International of justifying the acceleration of brutal capitalist contradictions in the name of socialist progress: "[o]ne reason why Fascism has a chance is that in the name of progress its opponents treat it as a historical norm."[4] During the course of the Chinese Revolution the "productive forces" analysis was understood as the position taken by the capitalist roaders, the camp of reaction that wanted to (and eventually succeeded in) derailing socialism by embracing capitalist logic.

6 Post-capitalist accelerationism is hampered by both its understanding of contradiction and its conception of acceleration. Its first error, an inability to grasp what is meant by core contradictions of capitalism, is quite easy to realize, particularly since the maxim to "accelerate the contradictions" is more of a pithy statement than a rigorous apprehension of the concrete. The belief that capitalism possesses contradictions that, when accelerated, will result in some form of socialism is a productive forces analysis of reality because it is based on some vague conception of "contradiction" that is not properly enunciated.

If capitalism possesses contradictions that stand in the way of socialism these are the following, interrelated axioms: i) over-accumulation and the limits of expansion; ii) forces of production in tension with obsolete relations of production; iii) the tension between irreconcilable social classes (bourgeois-proletariat) that drives the vicissitudes of this mode of production.

The first contradiction, which has been accelerated for a long time, is not one that, when reaching its imagined limits, will result in a humane post-capitalism. There are limits to the markets into which capitalism can expand, a limited amount of resources, but these are already offset, and have been for a long time, by the very nature of this contradiction: the ability of the mode of production to destroy what it creates, to generate "lack,"[5] the manic velocity in which this contradiction is already undermining the mode of production in a manner that leads towards barbarism rather than socialism: by sinking the most egregious affects of capitalist accumulation in the biosphere.

The second contradiction merely demonstrates the problem with post-capitalist accelerationism: the fact that the objective circumstances of productive forces are in contradiction with the subjective factor of productive relations—that there is no revolutionary movement to make the economic instance conform to the political—is not something that can be accelerated by capitalism. To assume that capitalism's core contradictions can be "accelerated" demonstrates very little understanding of contradiction: why should every contradiction possess a speed, why do these accelerationists imagine that capitalism defines this speed? Increased accumulation on the part of capitalism will not accelerate this contradiction; it will always persist, regardless of the speed of the reproduction of capital, as the limit of revolutionary transformation.

The third contradiction assumes that an acceleration of capitalism's contradictions will produce the subjective will to fight capitalism—that is, will transform the complacent worker-subject into the militant proletarian-subject. Such a position, though, ignores the fact that this subjective will is not magically called into being by objective circumstances, particularly since these objective circumstances (brutal, "austere" capitalism) are already the norm, and have been since capitalism's rosy dawn. The experience of these objective circumstances, even in the so-called "third world" or in 19th century Europe, have not by themselves necessitated the advent of a new revolutionary subject. Proletarianization may allow large sectors of the tiny minority of privileged workers to again connect with their militant heritage but this is not enough to produce revolution: at the most it will produce a radical trade union consciousness, the most militant articulation of reformist politics; at the least it will be sublimated in the ideology of austerity, inducing a docile acceptance of reified market ideology—that austerity policies are necessary for society's salvation.

Thus, post-capitalist accelerationism has little understanding of *contradiction*. As for its understanding of *acceleration*: the reactionary accelerationists better understand what is at stake and at least recognize that they are the enemies of progress. Capitalism is already accelerated and to endorse this acceleration is to endorse starvation, environmental devastation, and genocide.

7 The acceleration of capitalism's contradictions is precisely what the austerity apparatus promotes. On the surface this promise appears rather banal, particularly for those who occupy the top tiers of the global market and, from this privileged position, can argue that the seeds of post-capitalism are contained in its complete acceleration. But this acceleration, which has only been slowed down by welfare capitalism's state of social peace at the imperial metropoles, is not something that should ever be celebrated. For the majority of the world's population, for the exploited and oppressed masses, capitalism's natural state of velocity has always meant starvation, genocide, hellish work-houses, and ecocide. You accelerate the contradictions far enough and you end up with either a state of capitalist emergency (fascism) or environmental devastation.

We do not have to look very far to realize that accelerationism is also a position endorsed by the right. Nick Land and the "Dark Enlightenment" maintain similar positions except they are in some ways more aware of what this means: a whole-hearted embrace of capitalist reaction. And though they might kid themselves into believing that this acceleration will end capitalism so as to permit their pre-capitalist and Hobbesian state of affairs, this is because they are simply unaware that the world that they desire is not in contradiction with the capitalist horizon.

8 The greatest success of the austerity apparatus is in its ability to mobilize progressives in the acceptance of its narrative. If austerity is assumed to be inevitable, and a "kinder, gentler" capitalism impossible, then there will also be those who choose a siege mentality over even a reformist consciousness. On the one hand they recognize, though unconsciously, that a return to welfare capitalism is not a solution; on the other hand they believe that austerity is a fact, that the discourse generated by the apparatus is a natural law, and demand the most cowardly response to the current conjuncture: a siege mentality of damage control. Here we encounter sublimated forms of accelerationism.

"Art, Austerity, and the Production of Fear," an article that appeared in the arts and culture magazine *Fuse*, is a case in point.[6] Austerity policies have targeted the arts—understood as "frivolous" by honest capitalists who believe that good art will either be commodified or relegated to some vague patronage system—and the author chooses to accelerate the targeting by accepting it as fact and arguing that artists should adapt to the new reality of austerity. The fact that arts funding as a whole has not been axed entirely doesn't matter; they argue that this should already be accepted as a *fait accompli*, hastening austerity by terminating a popular magazine and suggesting that other artists involved in publicly funded zones embrace privatization, learning to survive creatively in the cracks of art austerity.

Another example: an executive member of a union local on strike arguing that the rank-and-file should ratify an insulting offer and return to work because, as long as capitalism exists, they cannot hope to achieve a better deal.[7] While it is indeed correct to recognize that the contradiction between labour and capital cannot be solved without the termination of the latter—and this executive member's argument adopted this radical language—such a claim is tantamount to saying: "austerity exists, we have to embrace the reality it proclaims!" All in the interest of a vague *strategy* that is about as strategic as building a bomb shelter and waiting for the world to end.

It is one thing to respond to austerity policies with a reformist strategy that aims to reestablish welfare capitalism as a norm; it is quite another to accept the "austere lifestyle" demanded by these policies, calling them progressive because of some incoherent communitarian justification. The former is a strategy that results from the way in which the austerity apparatus channels resistance into implicit collaboration. The latter is explicit collaboration.

9 Class struggle, the "protracted civil war" that determines the meaning of any and every mode of production, is thus that which the austerity apparatus seeks to repress. But as Freud has taught us—barring the idealist detours into his psychoanalysis—repression is never complete, only partially accomplished through sublimation and displacement. Being the basis of any and every social formation, class struggle cannot cease to exist (without, that is, either the elimination of classes or human societies), but it can be rendered invisible, suppressed to such an extent that the subject of austerity becomes convinced of its non-existence.

Since the state of social peace (welfare capitalism, an imperial detente between labour and capital) is that which the austerity apparatus seeks to normalize by making it the goal of all who challenge the reign of crisis capitalism, class struggle is repressed through this sublimation. And in the case of the state of emergency, which means the onslaught of fascism, this civil war will also be repressed: right populists are often adept at tricking the dangerous classes into adopting a substitute civil war—the *Volk* against the other.

10 Although the austerity apparatus cannot eradicate class struggle (to do so would be to eradicate the basis of the apparatus itself, class society), it functions to contain this protracted civil war. In times of crisis class struggle will become pointed as the violence beneath capitalism's supposed social peace is made apparent, but the austerity apparatus is that which manages crisis.

A labour disruption is always a moment of concrete class struggle. A strike, for example, is an event where workers are forced to recognize that their daily existence is in contradiction with that of their employers. At the moment of their emergence, however, these disruptions and strikes are only objective instances of class struggle. The point is to make them conscious of themselves, to turn them into subjective instances of class struggle where those involved become subjects militantly dedicated to struggling, as part of a larger class, against capitalism itself instead of capitalism's local ciphers—particular employers, bosses, managers, scabs. This means a shift from the economic to the political; economic struggle is given meaning by the opening of its political dimension.

The austerity apparatus works to contain class struggle by attempting to prevent this political dimension from manifesting. Economism is its goal, a regulation of class struggle according to the economic norms of capitalist society: a struggle only to meet immediate economic demands (the lower the better, of course!) rather than a struggle that develops, due to an interrogation of the economic instance, into a political struggle against capital.

Once again we are forced to recognize that the austerity apparatus is old wine in new skins. Ever since the historic concession between labour and capital, the enshrinement of trade-unionism within the (imperial) capitalist state of affairs, the potential for politicization has been managed by labour laws, legal union bodies, and bureaucrats. In these spaces, those who demand a return to "social unionism" or speak of politics beyond that which the rank and file are expected to demand are treated with suspicion and hostility.

11 The insidiousness of the austerity apparatus is in its ability to make traditional trade union consciousness masquerade as revolutionary consciousness. The ascendancy of business unionism has rendered social unionism (that is, the labour union ethos that treats the rank-and-file's decision making power as more significant than the official bureaucratic leadership) "radical" in comparison. In this context, the cunning of the austerity apparatus is to trick us into thinking that in these times of "austerity" an embrace of social unionism (a workerism from below) is the most revolutionary option. A forbidden option, but the only forbidden option. All that such a position signifies, though, is a return to trade union consciousness proper, as opposed to the petty-bourgeois consciousness fostered by the general state of the current labour movement in the imperial metropoles.

This return is not at all ideal for the austerity apparatus; its greatest successes, after all, are achieved by convincing first world workers to position themselves towards the state of emergency. The desire for this return is still part of the apparatus's everyday operations. For in some sense even social unionism, treated as an end in itself, signifies social peace: the union that has repositioned itself according to a social unionist ethos (which, in many ways, represents a desire to return to the labour unionism of the past) will still encounter the limits of economism. It may temporarily resist the extension of austerity policies into the heart of the working corps it represents, but only to be plugged back into the system as a whole: the contradiction between labour and capital will not be overstepped, only managed according to this radical local's success in striking to win. Win what? Surely not the end of capitalism. Only the survival of its workers within this mode of production.

While we must recognize that social unionism, and the proper trade union consciousness it mobilizes, is indeed necessary for any and every union struggle, we should not settle for such victories as the limit of class struggle. And this is precisely what the austerity apparatus demands: you've had your fun, you've won your demands, now back to work.

What we call "social unionism" was the normative way in which unions functioned in the past, and the way in which they still generally function outside of the imperialist metropoles. This has never been enough to make a labour union a "red union"—for such a transformation to be successful the influence of a revolutionary movement was always necessary. Unions, no matter how "social," cannot build themselves into revolutionary organizations by themselves: in the entire history of the labour union this has never been the case. It is necessary to grasp the gap between trade union and revolutionary consciousness in order to intervene against capital; the austerity apparatus attempts to prevent this recognition and thus dampens our ability to intervene.

notes

1. PCR-RCP, "Austerity: the Desperate Reflex of Capitalism in Agony" (www.pcr-rcp.ca/en/archives/1509)

2. Marx, *Capital vol. 1* (London: Lawrence & Wishart, 2003), 253.

3. Ibid., 282–283.

4. Walter Benjamin, *Illuminations* (New York: Shocken Books, 1968), 257.

5. In the sense meant by Deleuze and Guattari in *Anti-Oedipus* (Minneapolis: University of Minnesota Press, 1998) as "the presence of antiproduction within production itself" that produces "lack in the large aggregates, to introduce lack where there is always too much, by effecting the absorption of overabundant resources." (235) Think of big food companies who dump their grain into the oceans when they have too much to sell.

6. "Art, Austerity and the Production of Fear" (fusemagazine.org/2014/01/37-1_art-austerity-and-the-production-of-fear).

7. Here I am referring to a ratification meeting at the end of the first week of CUPE 3903's 2015 strike that resulted in the local being split with one unit ratifying and the other two units remaining on the picket lines. With the current state of the labour movement, however, this is only one of many examples.

on the state of affairs; the novelty of austerity

"...a living machinery, of clashing relationships to production, whose essential fuel is capital extracted by genocide, by slavery and dispossession and looting on a mass scale. Not as dead history, but right now."

Butch Lee and Red Rover, *Night-Vision*

1 A state of social peace, a state of anxiety, a state of emergency—these are all just positions of the state as a singular concept. We are thus still dealing with the theory of the capitalist state (capitalism as a general mode of production necessitates the political formation of the state) despite those odd attempts, from both bourgeois and "radical" theorists, to claim that the state is no longer conceptually relevant. In order to understand the austerity apparatus we need to reassert the order of the real: the capitalist state exists, and exists in multiple forms, and is not anachronistic; it mediates the imperial order in which the austerity apparatus is capable of operating.

2 All of this talk of Empire, initially popularized by Negri and Hardt, has succeeded in making the singular fact of the state appear obsolete. Although this is not the case—the state does exist and is relevant—there is still a rotting corpse of theoretical literature that would have us believe otherwise.

Empire deterritorializes. Empire is capitalism beyond the state. Empire has rendered borders and the centre-periphery distinction obsolete. Empire is some further development of capitalism, beyond imperialism, where the capitalist delirium of a market without borders—the lie of the invisible hand that every business student desperately wishes to believe—has been accepted as truth. "Unlike the modern State, which pretended to be an order of Law and Institutions, Empire is the *guarantor* of a reticular proliferation of norms and apparatuses. Under normal circumstances, Empire *is* these apparatuses."[1] But this is vague conjecture, nebulous theorizing that demonstrates an ignorance of what a state *is* and has *always been*: the modern state still exists, still functions as an order of law and institutions while, at the same time, guaranteeing this "reticular proliferation of norms and apparatuses"—the austerity apparatus being a recent example of one amongst many. The state also *is* these apparatuses inasmuch as any machine is the sum-total of the functions of its apparatuses.

Let us return to Lenin's definition of the state, the clearest and most concrete conceptualization. Although it is often deemed unfashionable to cite Lenin, this is because what is correct *is* quite often unfashionable, particularly if it comes from revolutionaries who initiated historic sequences that threatened the imperialist-capitalist order.

So from Lenin: the state is primarily a class dictatorship. That is, a machine for the suppression of one class by another. As long as there is class struggle there are *states* of class struggle, determined by those national boundaries that these machines call into being. To assume otherwise is to assume that there is no machine of class power, no class struggle, and the utopia of capitalism is complete. The state, being a machine of class suppression, does not simply *pretend* to be an order of law and institutions; the order of legality and institutional norms exists because of a given state and the apparatuses it necessitates as a machine of class power. If there is Empire then it is derived from the conglomerate of multiple states—some imperialist, some victims of imperialism—which is to say that there remains imperialism, commanded by the most powerful nation-states, and this is the order of the real.

3 A state is also a state of affairs. This is what a machine does: function so as to regulate a particular norm or norms. All machines have a definite function, no matter how complex their operations, something they do. A television is a machine designed to broadcast televised programming. A computer is a machine that computes data in a variety of ways. A state is a machine that suppresses, according to the limits of the mode of production, various classes. Such suppression is a state of affairs—that is, it produces a state of being, a particular reality—and there can be no state of affairs without a state machine. Those who deny the state deny the concrete because they cannot explain how and why business as usual functions. According to Empire? But this would also have to be a state of affairs and thus presuppose a state formation.

State of social peace, state of anxiety, state of emergency... these are simply various temperaments of the state of affairs. The machine of class management will sometimes be forced to make concessions so as to ensure its promulgation, occasionally worry about its fate, and always be ready to declare martial law. Consent: social peace. Coercion: emergency. And the nebulous state between: anxiety.

If we are to speak of an austerity apparatus we must first reckon with the persistence of the state, which will not vanish without the disappearance of class struggle, and understand how it is a component part of this machine of class suppression.

4 The austerity apparatus cuts across a variety of other apparatuses and operations in those states of affairs within which it functions. A meta-program, a series of redundant circuits, a parallel operation. A patchwork of multiple other apparatuses, austerity is yet another attempt to jury-rig an obsolete machine.

Due to its dispersal throughout those states in which it exists, it often becomes difficult to isolate its operation(s). In some ways it is a distinct apparatus, in other ways it is immanent to the already existing large-scale ideological apparatuses. We know it is a particular ideology, but we find it embedded in the state's instituted ideological submachines. We find it in the educational apparatus, the legal apparatus, the trade union apparatus. After all, the subjects who speak for these apparatuses are now also speaking of austerity according to its ideological limits.

5 If there is something new about the austerity apparatus it is not its policies that go by the name of "austerity" which are, as we have already discussed, essential to capitalism's business as usual. Its newness, or rather its novelty, concerns its operation as an ideological apparatus—the way in which it produces subject positions and a particular discursive framework about contemporary crisis capitalism. Here we use the term novel instead of new because we are still not dealing with an apparatus that is entirely unique but one that is a rearticulation of older and similar ideological apparatuses; the austerity apparatus is mainly a novel update of past attempts to reify capitalism in moments where its crisis limits produce states of anxiety.

Cobbled together from recycled parts of the state machinery, the austerity apparatus is akin to a "new" computer that has been assembled from cannibalized parts of old hardware. A novel device, new insofar as it didn't exist in this particular form before it was assembled; ultimately a second-hand clone complex, as old as its component parts.

6 The novelty lies in the discourse of austerity and the business of its apparatus. The concrete reason for the existence of this apparatus is not a new feature of capitalism: economic crisis is intrinsic to the mode of production. Once we look at the foundation upon which the apparatus rests, however, we do encounter something that is new, though something that was promised with the advent of capitalism: that this crisis, as predictable and similar as it might be, brings us closer to environmental collapse. If there is anything new in everything the apparatus obscures it is that we might be at that moment where the choice between socialism or barbarism is no longer a hypothesis derived from an understanding of capitalism's logic, but is viscerally imminent.

The discourse surrounding austerity, however, has been severed from what might actually be new; it is concerned only with the assumption that these policies enacted to save neoliberalism are unprecedented, when nothing can be further from the truth.

7 The novelty of the austerity apparatus was described in the first section: the way in which it operates to channel and redirect any opposition to capitalism itself towards this ideological thing called austerity. It is an apparatus that functions to force its ideology of austerity into the realm of the real—that reifies crisis capitalism by giving it the "phantom objectivity" of a supposed concrete thing called austerity—and, in doing so, produces subjects orientated around its pseudo-concreteness.

What makes this operation *novel* rather than properly *new* is that it is simply an update of past attempts, in other historical conjunctures where capitalism's essential crisis nature became evident (that is, when there was a state of anxiety that promised a state of emergency), that operated according to a similar definite function. In those states of anxiety in Europe, between the World Wars, broad swathes of the left found their energies redirected according to Bernstein's revisionist thesis that, in the face of crisis, attempted to normalize a social peace with capital. What they ended up endorsing, as we know, were multiple states of emergency: the rise of fascism. Halfway through the cold war history repeated as tragedy with Khrushchev's similar attempt to court social peace, but on a global scale, that did not even bother to hide its intent: peaceful co-existence with capital.[2]

The austerity apparatus produces similar subjects by remobilizing the same liberal sentiments, inherent to ruling class ideology: the desire for social peace, an amelioration of class struggle according to the terms dictated by capital, anxious creatures who hope to prevent emergency by re-valorizing the very thing upon which this emergency depends—the capitalist edifice itself. Austerity subjects are the same liberal subjects as before; their novelty lies in the fact that they imagine they are living in a new period of capitalism, that austerity is something that has never before been encountered, and in a very limited way they are correct: it is new insofar as it has been packaged to appear new, insofar as this "newness" is intrinsic to the novel way in which the austerity apparatus functions.

8 Novelty is not unimportant: it is the mutation of formal operations, the appearance of the new, of a machine that remains substantially the same. Automobiles and locomotives, for example, have gone through various formal transformations since their respective invention without, for all that, being anything more than novel adaptations.

Capitalism has therefore gone through various formal transformations—different in various regions and/or levels of operation—that have not altered its underlying logic. Each and every novel rearticulation has been a different way of confirming the same economic logic. Formally different states of affairs produced formally different subjects but, at the same time, these subjects shared a singular relationship.

When Marx and Engels first examined capitalism as a mode of production they were able to grasp its core logic despite the fact that it had only just achieved economic hegemony. Capitalism had not yet achieved political hegemony, though they had an inkling of this possibility in the various theories of ideology that they were able to propose. The incompleteness of these theories, later to be worked out by Gramsci and Althusser, was due to the fact that the bourgeois class was only beginning to grasp its consciousness and institute its values as common sense.

Neoliberalism, then, is merely that moment when capitalism achieved political hegemony, when the bourgeoisie's values became the measure of social reality. What we discover, here, is a unity between the economic and political after a period in which, at least in some regions of the world, the bourgeoisie was forced to make concessions to labour and prolong its economic hegemony by a social democratic aberration in the political sphere: welfare capitalism. Neoliberalism is a renewal of 19th century capitalism, but with a certain novel transformation of forces of production and social values, in which the attempted political hegemony of that time has finally become ascendant. People are beginning to consent to the logic of work-houses as the welfare state is eroded.

Simultaneously, outside of the imperialist metropoles (and even within its cracks) where the majority of the working poor reside, the economic order of 19th century capitalism has been the norm without, for all that, ideological consent.

The austerity apparatus emerges at that point where both the economic and political hegemony are facing crisis; it is an attempt to preserve this hegemony, particularly its political aspect, and thus the neoliberal state of affairs which is capitalism par excellence. It does this by promising the possibility of a period in which political hegemony was incomplete, a return to welfare capitalism—this is how it is also an apparatus of capture.

Hence, it is quite wrong when some argue that the state of emergency proposed by the austerity apparatus "looks less like capitalism than a variation on the Ancien Régime."[3] It resembles nothing more or less than capitalism itself.

9 Political theory is never tired of celebrating the new when, in point of fact, it has generally produced only the novel. Theories of biopower, Empire, rhizome, multitude, forms-of-life, and etc. sound compelling. They may even provide us with theoretical tools that are sometimes useful (though mainly in academic practice) for engaging with the world in which we live. Nevertheless, while it is rather unpopular to admit this truth in some circles, theory that falls outside of the Marxist sequence has largely been anticipated by this sequence. Moreover, many of these anticipations were superior to every alternate radical theory because they could provide greater explanatory depth and were (and are) the tools taken up in actual revolutionary practice.

A particular novelty of the austerity apparatus, which is of course part of its overall novelty, is that it has successfully mobilized the novel itself. By either rejecting the Marxist sequence or utilizing it in bad faith, a veritable army of radical intellectuals are designing new analyses to combat what they imagine to be a new development. To be fair, the historical development of capitalism *does* warrant the development of anti-capitalist theory: aside from the obvious fact that manufacture, the working day, imperialism, forces of production, and many other capitalist characteristics have changed since the times of Marx or Lenin, most of us are familiar with the kind of Marxist who thinks that there has been no relevant theoretical development since 1917—a rather unimaginative lot, incapable of thinking through the problematics of the current state of affairs.

Admitting the development of capitalism's formal aspects and demanding that Marxist theory evolve according to this development, however, is not the same as either embracing a *new* theory or pretending that the contemporary conjuncture does not pose new challenges. A return to this sequence, though, is something that the austerity apparatus, as a novel liberal apparatus par excellence, attempts to bar. It is less threatened by novel theoretical discourses; it encourages eclecticism.

10 While it is correct to recognize that the economic crisis that began in the early 2000s is unique insofar as it is the first truly "global crisis and not regional,"[4] it is wrong to assume that the mechanisms of austerity are as new as the crisis they seek to command. The ideology that attempts to navigate an economic crisis is less unique than the crisis itself, and much contemporary theory wastes its time in conflating the unique aspects of the crisis with the less unique, but entirely novel, aspects of ideological containment. Austerity is not crisis but has functioned as a stand-in for crisis—which is why we often waste time speaking of austerity, and not the crisis, as the material foundation for the current conjuncture when we are in fact looking at a world in reverse. Today's crisis, an immanence grasped by Marx and Engels the moment they conceptualized a world market, produces novel variants of ideological containment that are similar to past strategies—what we now call austerity. Unfortunately, austerity is often misconstrued as being the foundation of crisis: hence these strange assumptions that a creditor-debtor contradiction has replaced the contradiction of capital-labour, that neoliberalism is a complete rupture with liberalism, and that we need to invent entirely new categories to explain the crisis in particular assemblages of ruling class hegemony.

Every crisis challenges the way in which ruling class hegemony is internally configured. Austerity measures, even if they did not use this name in the past, were mobilized in bourgeois internecine struggles: we can locate narratives about "thriftiness" and the "sin of excessive spending" in past crises; we can discover a struggle between ruling class factions in the discourse of the plutocrat. A challenge to the internal configuration of ruling class hegemony, however, is not a challenge to its hegemony as a class. And today's austerity apparatus hopes to convince us that, whatever problems the crisis causes, this hegemony is not also in crisis.

notes

1. Tiqqun, *Introduction to Civil War* (Los Angeles: Semiotext[e], 2010), 134.

2. But reactionaries are never satisfied with the attempts of an anxious left to court social peace. In these states of anxiety, after all, the reactionary will always demand an embrace of some form of emergency, of monolithic capitalism. While we anti-revisionists treated Khrushchev's theory of "peaceful co-existence" as betrayal, this was still not acceptable for the capitalist reactionary who can never tolerate an anxious subject facing in the direction of social peace rather than emergency. Hence, in order to isolate his liberal opponents who were content with the Soviet Union's policy of non-aggression and embrace of social peace, that arch-reactionary Reagan would argue that Khrushchev's demand for "peaceful co-existence" was a conspiracy designed to undermine the manifest destiny of capitalism to obliterate anything that obstructed the market.

3. Maurizio Lazzarato, *Governing By Debt* (South Pasadena: Semiotext[e], 2015.), 10.

4. Christian Marazzi, *The Violence of Financial Capitalism* (Cambridge: Semiotext[e], 2011), 13.

a crisis in hegemony; a crisis in security

"Security functions… as a tautology of onto-political crisis, gaining currency from ongoing images of emergency and disorder that must be met with continual attention and intervention."

Colleen Bell, *The Freedom of Security*

1 Consider the manner in which bourgeois ideology in its most "humane" form (that is, liberalism) became common sense. Hundreds of years of a class that would become the bourgeoisie struggling, and often quite violently, to secure its hegemony pre-existed the establishment of what is now understood as liberal humanism, enshrined in J.S. Mill's *On Liberty*: free speech, utilitarian calculus, the market of ideas.

The French Terrors were the most radical expression of the bourgeois order, particularly since they required the support of the popular masses to establish this order: the great chain of being needed to be suppressed so that the bourgeois order could supersede the divine right of kings. And though reactionaries such as Edmund Burke were horrified by the onslaught of this new political sequence, they were quite wrong in their complaint about revolutions eating their own children: these moments of violence and class suppression contributed to the hegemony necessary *to produce children*—bourgeois and liberal subjects who saw themselves as individuals outside of the chain of being. The eating would come later, as part of the new mode of production called into being, and had to do with the economic order, rather than the confused political sequence of revolutions that helped establish this order. For if these revolutions had devoured their children then the bourgeois subject would have also been cannibalized and capitalism would have never emerged.

The English Civil War also produced its subjects, and the most conservative articulation of the new sequence—the position represented by Hobbes—was foundational to liberal ideology. Forget for a moment that Hobbes demanded, in the face of the "war of all against all," the absolute state. What was the logic behind this demand? The ideology of the bourgeois liberal subject: individuals locked in competition in a state of nature where right conflicted with right. The Leviathan is justified by nascent capitalist ideology and Hobbes's absolute state simply prefigures the contemporary state of emergency: the monolithic state is justified by the assumption of a liberal subject. If anything, Hobbes indicates the history behind the emergence of modern and "humane" bourgeois liberalism: bourgeois power needed to first be absolute before it could relax and allow for the "free expression" endorsed by Mill.

Hundreds of years before the bourgeois state emerges as *fait accompli*, but we like to pretend that capitalism was always opposed to censorship, was essentially democratic, and promoted free expression. Mill's *On Liberty* is written only after this long sequence, after capitalism has achieved hegemony.

Centuries of class war, wherein the bourgeois class asserted its dominance by repressing the aristocracy, preceded this articulation of the liberal subject. And Mill *admits this truth* when he claims, at various points in his treatise, that it was necessary to reign in individual excesses so as to prevent the modern state from devolving into chaos.

Now modern liberalism is presented to us as a fact of nature, as if it appeared immediately the moment that capitalism was formed, and that we should recognize free expression as essential to the liberal capitalist order. We are supposed to forget a history in which pre-Millsian liberals treated all of these so-called "liberal" values as obstructions to the free market.[1] Even worse, we are supposed to forget that this political order of free expression was only possible after centuries wherein the bourgeois class pursued hegemony by suppressing its class enemies—both those above and those below—so as to establish itself as the ruling class with ruling ideas that, in this establishment, would become common sense. How is this common sense even achieved? By violently making oneself into the ruling class through both the deposition of prior ruling classes and the violent suppression of the popular classes that helped with this deposition: the English Civil War, the French Revolution with both the Terrors and the Haitian Slave

Revolution, the far more conservative American War of Independence (a secession that functioned primarily to *suppress* the popular classes of the slaves and ensure bourgeois order), and everything in between. Competing classes were suppressed, a counter-hegemony was established so as to produce total hegemony of the bourgeois order.

Whence comes Mill? After this class hegemony has been achieved: it is easy to speak about free speech in a context where the normative subject is one who is primed to think according to the bourgeois order. Before Mill's time suppression was required; the Hobbesian absolute state was needed to make bourgeois ideology the ruling ideology. Once this ideology had succeeded in becoming common sense, the tradition of Millsian liberalism could manifest to speak about the importance of free speech and the marketplace of ideas. After all, once the ruling ideas of the ruling class are enshrined as common sense—once the bourgeoisie achieved complete hegemony—there is no point in worrying about whether counter-ideas will threaten this hegemony. As long as this counter ideology is not backed by action: Mill's "corn dealer" example is a case in point—just as long as communists only publish their ideas in books and tracts, rather than assembling as a class to challenge their class enemy, business as usual can continue. We are meant to forget that the social order defended by Mill's liberalism only came into being by the kind of violent suppression he attempts to banish to the past.

2 Long before the emergence of the austerity apparatus the liberal subject was normative. Before the so-called "age of austerity" it was often commonplace for would-be radicals, regardless of their supposed commitment to anti-capitalism, to assume that the high point of the liberal order was a fact of nature. To treat the marketplace of ideas as essential to political discourse, to argue according to its logic of censorship and anti-censorship, and assume that politics was contained in proper debate rather than class struggle. This is the genius of liberal ideology: it is able to incorporate dissent into its broad network of hegemony; it can accept dissent so long as this dissent can be commodified and neutralized. That which is hegemonic has no fear of challenging ideas, just so long as these ideas remain at the level of free speech rather than dissenting action: in the latter case the repressive arm of the state will manifest, and often justify its manifestation according to liberal principles—the freedom of the capitalist needs to be protected against the freedom of labour, as if these two sites of freedom are equal.

Before capitalism consummated its hegemony this kind of freedom was impossible; the class that is currently in command needed to consummate the order of its command. Now, having succeeded in socializing consent to its ideology, alternate perspectives can be allowed because these alternate perspectives are often relegated to the realm of opinions.

We often treat this order as always-and-ever complete, as if it never engaged in a violent struggle to achieve hegemony. In the face of its supposed excesses we think it is entirely moral to abide by its rule of law without grasping how it became a rule of class law in the first place: by enforcing a state of affairs in which its ruling class suppressed other classes so as to enshrine itself as *the* ruling class. What's more, for the liberal subject it becomes rather easy to ignore the fact that enemy classes are still being suppressed and that naked violence is commonplace for most of the world's population.

Even when we witness this violence the power of bourgeois ideology is such that we imagine that we are witnessing excesses, "states of exception" rather than the most viscerally concrete operations of the bourgeois order.

3 In this age of austerity, as with any moment of capitalist crisis, existence is simultaneously experienced as a crisis of security. Social peace with capital crumbles; a state of emergency becomes imminent. The ravages of a failing system begin to disrupt spontaneous consent to bourgeois rule as the values of the ruling class become questionable—even the culture industry makes a buck by promulgating distrust for the so-called 1%. The coercive aspect of the state manifests to enforce consent: the most unruly elements of the rabble, as ever, are beaten and jailed—a normative experience for those outside of the imperial metropoles, as well as those colonized and super-exploited populations within; the confused and anxious are socialized to consent to an increase of coercive apparatuses (surveillance, a larger and more disciplined police force, counter-insurgency, etc.) in a space that once believed itself free from the repressive wing of the state.

4 The ruling class security discourse is possessed by a cynical irony: capitalism is responsible, particularly during crisis, for producing the worst forms of insecurity (lack of access to food, housing, safety, clean water, etc.) and yet attempts to secure the continuation of this insecurity through increased militarization that it labels security. Security for the ruling class and its lackeys, yes, but not for the vast majority of the world's population. Robert Biel has investigated this contradiction to a significant degree, noting that:

> The ruling order builds its credentials on combating insecurity on behalf of society, on rebuilding the structure which the era of unpredictability dissolves. To do so, it claims exceptional (extraordinary) repressive powers. The notion of 'terrorism' is convenient in conjuring up everyone's nameless fears of some threatening or chaotic force. In the United States, you have more *real* risk of being killed by a law-enforcement officer than by a terrorist, [...] but *the discourse turns this reality upside down, such that capitalism's own failure becomes the justification for an entrenchment of its dominance.* As a result, the whole debate which should be about a solution to crisis becomes siphoned into building the repressive apparatus.[2]

In the age of austerity the masses experience real insecurity; the austerity apparatus functions to convince these masses to accept the very coercion that promotes this insecurity in the name of its opposite. From the perspective of the ruling class, however, the promotion of widespread insecurity means security for the state of affairs. Hence, as Colleen Bell has indicated in her masterful examination of security discourse, "the politics of security are organized around the management of the population and the promotion of suitable forms of life to the exclusion of other forms."[3]

5 The security of the ruling class has always been a concern of the capitalist state of affairs; all class societies must produce state apparatuses that protect the dominance of the class in command. What we are now observing at the height of today's crisis—the so-called age of austerity—is, again, a novel articulation of what has been intrinsic to this social system from its very beginning, just as it has been intrinsic to the reproduction of previous modes of production. Moreover, those at the peripheries of global capitalism (including the peripheries within the imperial metropoles) have consistently experienced the coercive aspect of the system. A crisis merely extends the sphere of coercion, moving it from these supposed "states of exception" (which are, in fact, not exceptions but, for the majority of the world, the norm) to the heart of the system where the consensual aspect of the system is usually ascendant.

The Occupy movement, for example, demonstrated that large segments of the US "middle class," the scions of those populations who traditionally accepted bourgeois values as common sense, were no longer willing to consent to the state of affairs. Despite its inability to move beyond the limits of petty-bourgeois rebellion, it would still be inaccurate to conceptualize the Occupy movement as entirely petty-bourgeois, as some have done. There was an element of possible proletarianization: a formerly privileged population was forced, by the crisis, into recognizing the limits of an order that it might have accepted—*that it might have consented to*—in a period of capitalist stability.

6 Capitalism has always contained an element of coercive security beneath the security gleaned from social consent. The Hobbesian state of nature has always lurked at the margins of class hegemony: a chaotic revolt against the ruling class misconceived as a war of all-against-all... because, if the bourgeois order is treated as reality itself, then every rebellion, spontaneous or otherwise, will be treated as a war of the unruly masses against the all of a total reality.

Hence, the liberal order contains the germ of a state of emergency. The free market cannot enforce spontaneous consent for eternity. This liberal delirium disintegrates the moment we are confronted with a possible world where people can choose, in a space where ideological hegemony is in question, a different state of affairs.

Behind Rawls's "veil of ignorance" would the rational agent, once stripped of any awareness of class fidelity, truly be self-interested? The fact that Rawls rigged his thought experiment according to the ideology of welfare capitalism—that is, the Keynesianism that was popular during his time—is less interesting than the possibility that, if we really took his thought experiment at its word, rational agents rendered unconscious of their social positions ought to have no interest in accepting any system where these social positions were consciously enshrined. Better to enforce the persistence of this market through state intervention than allow for individuals to rationally choose a better state of affairs. Not that they would be able to do this, of course, but libertarians seem to imagine that their free market order's viability is premised on the rational choices of individuals freed from state repression: a version of the Rawlsian thought experiment stripped of its unexamined fidelity to capitalist ideology simply demonstrates that without the intervention of the capitalist state of affairs—including all of its ideological force—there would be no rational reason for individuals to spontaneously consent to free market domination.

Forget the thought experiment: in this age of austerity the state is consistently injecting public resources into the private sector and finance capital. The bail-outs in 2008–2009 (the Emergency Economic Stabilization Act) should have been enough to convince us that the state will close ranks to protect the economic order that provided it with life.

Hence now in USAmerica, with the election of Trump in 2016, the state of emergency is emergent and the liberal order has (as it has historically done with all fascisms) enabled this emergence. The same liberals who decried the fascism of Trump and the "alt-right" so as to shame leftists to vote for the worst neoliberal now shame these same left-ists for violently confronting fascists in the street. Moreover, this state of emergency crawled out of a liberal order that imposed this state upon New Afrikans, immigrants, and Indigenous nations for years. In the year leading up to the election it was open season on New Afrikans with Obama's regime defending a "Blue Lives Matter" campaign instead of the Black Lives Matter movement. In the six months before the election the army was unleashed upon Lakota militants in South Dakota.

7 The austerity apparatus, however, possesses a novel function in the realm of security. So as to breathe new life into a failing machine, it channels the energy of its subjects towards a consent of coercion. It is not enough that the state's repressive apparatus needs to intervene to consolidate capitalist hegemony; the austerity apparatus overdetermines this intervention into an acceptance of security in the midst of insecurity. Here we find the security discourse working "through the political endowments and capacities of the population, promoting desirable forms of conduct and enlisting the citizenry in the management of risks."[4] The instability produced by capitalism generates a response the austerity apparatus hopes to capture and mediate: channeling the energy of its subjects either back into the possibility (which might be forever blocked) of social peace, or towards a state of emergency.

If these subjects have been forced to become the risk-takers of this period of crisis, as Lazzarato suggests, then they might indeed believe that the solution to their problems, whether these are their failed mortgages, student loans, credit card payments, etc., lies in a capitalist state of affairs that absorbs debt. Some, however, might choose the reactionary path, blame convenient scape-goats for their malaise ("it was the immigrants stealing our jobs"), and gravitate towards a state of emergency where capitalism will close ranks and enshrine a militant top-down security practice. Fascist/isolationist solutions, such as the Reagan-era "Fortress America," are still promoted as armageddonist solutions to the age of austerity. And now in regions such as the US, with the election of Trump, these state of emergency solutions are being taken.

The fascist armageddon does not come from nowhere; it is merely one expression of the capitalist state of affairs, the elements of which were inherent in this mode of production since the beginning.

notes

1. For an excellent examination of the "illiberalism" of liberalism, see Jeff Noonan's *Democratic Society and Human Needs* (Kingston: McGill-Queen's University Press, 2006).

2. Robert Biel, *The Entropy of Capitalism* (Chicago: Haymarket Books, 2012), 169, our emphasis.

3. Colleen Bell, *The Freedom of Security* (Vancouver: University of British Columbia Press, 2011), 25.

4. Ibid., 39.

on the austerity subject; anxiety

"... the subject becomes inaugurated at the moment when the social power that acts on it, that interpellates it, that brings it into being through these norms is successfully implanted within the subject itself and when the subject becomes the site of the reiteration of these norms, even through its own psychic apparatus."

Judith Butler, *Changing the Subject*

1 The austerity apparatus has produced its own subject. The austerity subject, the capitalist social being whose social consciousness is determined by the operations of the apparatus that called it into existence. The austerity subject accepts the state of anxiety as a fact of nature and believes that its solution is found either in emergency or social peace. The austerity subject is either fascist or social democrat... And here again we find historical precedent: there was a time where social democrats were indeed called social fascists. It's really the same subject; only its stance, the state of affairs towards which it faces (peace or emergency?), determines its consciousness. Sometimes the formal difference between stances might appear significant—those demanding a return to welfare capitalism in the face of austerity are different than those who embrace austerity—but other times these formal differences are minuscule: those who accept austerity as inevitable, while complaining about this inevitability, will propose activities that parallel the stance of the most fascist variant of the austerity subject.

2 The austerity subject is not a total subject but only a facade that is cobbled together from the ideological detritus accumulated by the day-to-day functioning of the austerity apparatus. It is a subject position, rather than a subject that possesses complete unification between being and consciousness, that over codes other subjectivities that lurk within capitalism as a whole. Hence, it can be both the liberal and conservative subject, the rebellious and faithful subject, the would-be communist and the crypto-fascist. Contradictions abound: the austerity apparatus is such that, as a jury-rigged machine, it is never able to produce total fidelity to its operations; at best it can only paper over contradictions and pull already-existing subjects into its orbit.

The machine produces a normative subjectivation, but no subjection is total; there is always something within every human being that remains underdetermined. And the normative subjectivation of the austerity apparatus is even less complete than other subject-orders because, at this stage in the capitalist state of affairs, it is becoming difficult for the entire system to maintain its hegemony. Following the financial crisis, even at the imperialist metropoles, capitalist values are becoming less-and-less "common sense." When even the culture industry is forced to refer, though in a distorted form, to successful capitalists as out of touch, or as parasitical "1%-ers," it becomes increasingly obvious that the contradictions are becoming apparent and the valuation of ruling class hegemony is no longer popular.[1]

The subject position produced by the austerity apparatus is one that, if it does recognize the limitations of the entire system, will remain within the orbit of this machine despite its complaints. It is an austere position because it strictly limits its behaviour to the boundaries imposed by the system, the boundaries the austerity apparatus intends to protect.

3 The inauguration of the austerity subject is necessarily incomplete. All subject inaugurations are, in a sense, incomplete because there is something about the material grounds of human being that will resist subjectivation, that will find itself caught between multiple sites of subjectivity. There is no point in working this problematic out here, aside from pointing out that if we are materialists we must accept that humans, as a species, are different from kelp. What matters is simply this point: the austerity subject is not inaugurated in the same manner as other subjects because its interpellation is caught within a vacillation between a state of social peace and a state of emergency. It is a subject unsure of itself; this is both its strength and weakness.

4 The austerity apparatus treats the end result of the liberal sequence as normative, as the basis upon which its subject is founded. Part of its novelty lies in its ability to reify this liberal sequence by producing subjects who imagine they are experiencing processes and policies that are illiberal when, in point of fact, the austerity subject is a particular kind of liberal subject. If she faces towards the state of emergency then she does so in the manner of Hobbes, one of the founders of liberal thought. If she faces towards the state of social peace then she confirms the kind of liberal-ism exemplified by Mill or Rawls. If she critiques the state of emergency but is still convinced that the age of austerity is more than an ideological apparatus then she has accepted precisely what a liberal subject is meant to accept: that capitalism possesses moments of unexpected excess, alarming mutations that "change everything" and force us to imagine we are in a different political order that demands a new political theory.

5 While it is correct to recognize the ways in which neoliberal concepts of debt and credit have informed the austerity subject, it is incorrect to assume that this subject is simply, as Lazzarato claims, the indebted man. For Lazzarato, who has thoroughly interrogated the genealogy of debt and credit that is part of the neoliberal order, "[d]ebt constitutes the most general power relation through which the neoliberal power bloc institutes class struggle... [i]t immediately acts at the global level, affecting entire populations, calling for and contributing to the ethical construction of the indebted man."[2] In a later book he claims that the working class no longer exists as a class, "marginalized" by debt-credit capitalism, fragmented by a debt-credit class struggle and thus prevented from being a "political class."[3]

What Lazzarato is noticing is the existence of the austerity subject which is more than a subject defined by debt—it is a subject defined by all of the novel processes of the age of austerity, of which debt (also novel since it existed before in a different form) is only one aspect. Moreover, he is grasping only the subject that is demanded by the austerity apparatus, a subject which is intended *not* to be a political class. More accurately: a subject which is socialized and disciplined so as to reject class consciousness.

On the concrete level of class what is actually happening during this moment of crisis—the very thing the austerity apparatus intends to prevent by producing a particular subjectivation—is the possible reproletarianization of a first world working class.[4] In order to prevent the masses from recognizing themselves as proletarian (that is, as a political class), the austerity subject is constructed and valorized. None of this means that the political class does not potentially exist, just that it might not exist *for itself*.

Again we are forced to recognize that this is merely a novel deployment of subject-production: capitalism has always had ideological apparatuses that functioned so as to prevent the working class from recognizing itself as a political class; it is an error to mistake these top-down subjectivations as proof of the non-existence of the proletarian-bourgeois antimony that forms the basis of revolutionary class struggle. We will return to this theme in a later section.

6 The austerity subject, be it progressive or reactionary, seeks solidarity on the basis of austerity ideology. A subject requires solidarity so as to be a subject; it demands that others recognize the state of anxiety upon which its social being, and thus its consciousness, is dependent. Let us dismiss, for the moment, the reactionary variant of this subject who attempts to enforce solidarity by demanding the unqualified acceptance of the "age of austerity" and the supposed necessity of contemporary crisis capitalism's reforms: tighten your belts, forget class struggle, learn to adapt—anyone who has bothered to read this far most probably rejects this approach to reality. Here, our concern is with the radical austerity subject whose confirmation of austerity lies in their very rejection of austerity.

With austerity proffered as the primary enemy, solidarity is understood as that which challenges austerity policies regardless of the politics of this challenge. Austerity becomes a stand-in for capitalism itself; the united front becomes the limit of radicalism. There was a time when radicals spoke of three weapons necessary for the struggle against capitalism: the united front, the people's army, and the revolutionary party. The austerity subject elevates the united front to the level of primacy and, in doing so, intentionally obliterates the other weapons—or, more accurately, imagines that these other weapons are accomplished in its united front. A vast coalition to end austerity will serve as a substitute for both a people's army *and* a revolutionary party: it will become both of these things because a coordinated attack on austerity is understood, by the radical austerity subject, as the consummation of revolutionary politics. Hence Syriza, which was nothing more than a united front coalesced around anti-austerity, was misconceived as a revolutionary party; it was a stand-in for a people's army because it was articulated as the expression of the Movement of Squares.

This kind of solidarity brooks no opposition. All political critiques are dismissed as either "sectarian" or silencing. And the fact that all political movements that have been effective were misconstrued as "sectarian" simply because they were principled, or as "silencing" because any coherent politics must draw clear lines of demarcation, should be telling.

The austerity apparatus, though, demands fidelity. If it must foster radical subjects then it will channel them towards the state of social peace and, in doing so, convince them to silence their opposition according to the very complaint of silencing.

7 The austerity subject, no matter which direction they face, is a scornful subject, disdainful of militant politics. In its most radical articulation this subject will openly proclaim a militant politics but this is just a costume, a moribund and academic dedication. The politics that someone proclaims is not always the politics they practice in their everyday life: one can easily be left in form and right in essence.

This gap between theory and practice is not difficult to recognize: just look for the loudest self-proclaimed communist (or anarchist) who can't even manage a commitment to trade union consciousness. Look for the "radical" windbag who tells workers to accept concessions for "strategic" reasons and complains about how the bosses are "dividing" the workers simply because one faction of workers recognizes that another is on the side of the bosses. What is going on, however, is that there were pre-existing divisions between factions of workers; to make them apparent *is* to attack the bosses, to draw politically demarcating lines.[5] Someone who fails to be radical even within the limits of economism is also someone, regardless of his rhetoric, who will fail to be radical in the larger, political sense. If you fall far below the standard of trade union consciousness, you cannot pretend that you possess a revolutionary consciousness.

Solidarity with social peace or emergency: this is the subject community of austerity. A community that, in solidarity with capital *in concrete practice*, attempts to discipline those who reject this community for being poor sports.

8 For the austerity subject who wears left clothing, the practice of militant politics is frightening. Anything that draws lines of demarcation so as to enforce a political order violates the solidarity of the same that the austerity subject, who is always a liberal subject, desires to enforce.

This austerity subject might even go so far as to define all militancy as "fascist" since, unaware that a fascist subject is closer to their position than they imagine, they mistake fascism as anything and everything that is illiberal. Of course fascism, being its own radical political order (a radical political order of reaction) will also and militantly draw demarcating lines; this is why, when it is pursued by conscious fascist subjects, it is effective—it knows what it is doing, it pursues its politics in a committed and coherent manner.[6] But fascism has also required liberal subjects who, in their desire to enforce a given state of affairs, are too anxious to combat it with anti-fascist militancy. Moreover, as noted, the austerity subject who embraces the state of emergency *is* the fascist subject.

Concerned with prolonging the system as it is, regardless of whatever dream horizon of socialism they might proclaim, the austerity subject, always and ever an anxious subject, would prefer to lurk at the level of sober debate, the terms of which were established by the austerity apparatus.

9 Being an anxious subject, the austerity subject's fascist position is as qualified as its social democratic position. Affected by a default liberalism it is only fascist insofar as it faces the fascist solution to the state of anxiety in which it finds its subjective meaning. Its fascism is apologetic, a pretence at not being fascist just as its progressive variant pretends it does not really endorse a state of social peace. Still worried by social commitments, concerned more with damage control than the endorsement of a coherent political line, the austerity subject who faces the state of emergency also claims that this position is one of realism, the only solution to the crisis-as-state-of-nature.

Take, for example, the lukewarm supporters of Greece's Golden Dawn who, in a slightly embarrassed manner, pretend they don't *actually* support the Golden Dawn but only its analysis of the crisis. Claiming that they aren't "really fascists" they still endorse, despite trying to curtail their choice of words, the state of emergency promised by a committed fascist movement.

A micro-fascism: the austerity subject is always uncomfortable with explicit commitment.

10 The normative anxiety of the austerity subject is due to the fact that the age of austerity is simultaneously an age of anxiety. The state of anxiety, after all, is the state that capitalist machines enter during moments of crisis: the welfare state, dependent on imperialist equilibrium, suddenly discovers that its stability is not eternal and desperately desires this stability to return despite a crisis that is revealing that its order is built on sand. The solution is either a return to the social democracy promised by welfare capitalism or the monolithic capitalism promised by fascism—both the state of social peace and the state of emergency are moments of capitalist stability.

In this age of anxiety, commonplace at the imperialist metropoles experiencing crisis, the austerity subject is a cipher for liberal confusion. After decades of being socialized and disciplined according to imperialist privilege and the culture industry, anxiety emerges from the cracks opened by crisis. A worry that things cannot continue in the same manner, that something must be done to save the belle époque.

Hence the austerity apparatus and its subjective order. The middle-ground between emergency and social peace is opened, a confused and vague epistemological universe where both fascism and welfare capitalism are equally possible and not-possible. A commitment to nothing but capitalism's destined austerity which can mean, simultaneously, a fight for a return to social peace or a descent into emergency. If the austerity apparatus and its subjects attempt to keep this middle way hegemonic for as long as possible it is only because the state of emergency is slowly appearing more appealing the longer all attempts to reinstate social peace result in dismal failures.

Out of anxiety, governments debate about if and when to institute procedures associated with states of emergency (i.e. surveillance and anti-terrorist laws, criticism of the police as "hate speech"), and out of the same anxiety citizens hem-and-haw about the possible curtailment of civil liberties, but eventually the possibility of these laws creeps into the state of affairs. Anxious subjects complain but adapt.

The austerity apparatus promotes the new normal; its subjects anxiously acclimatize.

11 The root of the state of anxiety is the chaos implicit in this period of capitalist crisis. When this chaos, the result of capitalism's current state of entropy, is apprehended by the austerity subject the only response is anxiety. In some ways a return to the state of social peace is forbidden due to the point reached by capitalism's decay—such a state of affairs would be qualified, the environmental devastation will not allow such a perfect return. In other ways, the reactionary desire for a state of emergency will not resemble the fascisms of old: the contemporary states of emergency, an anxious possibility, will be armageddon fascisms, what Biel has called exterminism, where entropic chaos is embraced and a privileged few kept safe in gated communities.

What is most significant about this state of anxiety and its chaotic/entropic foundation is the denial that allows for the austerity subject to perceive chaos in an anxious rather than terrified manner. "Denial has thus become crucial to the system's mode of operation."[7] Denial that capitalism possesses clear limits, that its logic demands environmental collapse, is part of the everyday functioning of the austerity apparatus: this is, after all, an apparatus that functions to deny the limits of capitalism by imposing limits on its subjects. Such a denial worms its way into the heart of the austerity subject who, faced with the obvious excesses of capitalism, is being conditioned to apprehend capitalism's entropy as a moment of anxiety.

12 If it did not take very long for the austerity apparatus to transform the average capitalist subject into an austerity subject, this is because capitalism has always disciplined its subjects into accepting adaptation to its internal mutations. The ruling ideas of the ruling class are such that, when understood as a mirror of common sense values, all variations can be incorporated into the average subject as a matter of course, translated by degree into the next articulation of common sense.

The pressures produced by crisis capitalism did not happen overnight, though sometimes the crisis erupted in unexpected ways, and decades of ideological discourse that anticipated this age of austerity were already part of the ideological constellation. Years of casualization and precarity preceded (and contributed to) the ideology of austerity; long before this, at the "rosy dawn of capitalism," what we now call austerity was part of the "natural order."[8] With such a history, it should be no surprise that the capitalist subject came into existence with some ur-form of austerity at the heart of its being. All justifications for its existence were already made in the 18th and 19th centuries; the austerity apparatus is simply reoperationalizing old ideological reticulations. These are compelling because we have accumulated them into our consciousness simply by living and breathing the stench of senile capitalism.

13 What some have called the culture industry, or what others have called spectacle, has permitted this adaptation: entire technologies and cultural products exist so as to acclimatize us to the internal vicissitudes of a reality limited by capitalism's horizons. The anxious subject—the austerity subject—was already being disciplined mechanically by the fragmented social media technologies that emerged just before the austerity apparatus was assembled.

Comment strings on Facebook and blogs filled with trolls, arguments that go nowhere, anxious and arrogant ruminations. Twitter announcements that are confined to statements of emergency. Tumblr postings comprised of disconnected critiques. Messaging and smart-phones that produce chasms of social space in the same room. A vast channeling of energy; the production of the internet radical, the political subject whose revolutionary credentials are no more and no less than online participation.

While it is correct to note that these social media technologies are useful for counter-hegemonic agitation—and like any technology produced by capitalism, *can* be used progressively—we would be remiss if we failed to recognize the way in which they were intended to function as part of the culture industry: the way in which they fragment the subject and produce anxiety; the way in which they convince this very same subject that its liberation will be operationalized primarily within the very technologies that now function so as to galvanize the anxiety that is necessary for the austerity subject.

The ideology of the social media revolution and crowd-sourcing in some ways prevents concrete revolutionary struggle and thus generates a legitimate outlet for the most "radical" elements of the austerity subject. The point, here, is to disconnect social media from social struggle and produce a discourse in which it is accepted as fact that social struggle can only operate within the framework of social media where anxiety is the norm. The austerity apparatus has always sought to channel rebellion into "legitimate" avenues of expression.

Is it any wonder that these technologies crystallized during this economic crisis, just before the "age of austerity" was declared? Crisis produces anxiety at the privileged metropoles (at the peripheries, misery is predominant); anxious technologies—both a pseudo-solution and a reinforcement of this anxiety—refocus our attention from the cause of this state. To discipline a particular subject order. Pundits tell us that a period of anxiety is the result of texting, Twitter, Facebook, smart-phones, but as with everything in the age of austerity these are simply novel symptoms of the crisis that is intrinsic to the fundamental operations of capitalism.

notes

1. Popular television shows and movies may occasionally demonstrate disdain for ruling class values. At the same time, these are multi-million dollar productions. The fact that a disdain for the values behind the culture industry can be enunciated by the culture industry itself demonstrates one of the Frankfurt School's concerns about this industry: the ability to see through the terms of one's oppression/exploitation but accept these terms in the very practice of production. This understanding of the culture industry, in some ways, defines the day-to-day operations of the austerity apparatus: we see the problems of capitalism but channel our energy back into the very thing that produces these problems, thus providing an acceptance to the basis of austerity.

2. Maurizio Lazzarato, *The Making of the Indebted Man* (Los Angeles, Semiotext[e], 2012), 89.

3. Ibid., *Governing by Debt* (South Pasadena, Semiotext[e], 2015), 12–13.

4. The concept of "reproletarianization" has a long history. For our purposes we can find conceptual precedence in Christopher Day's "reproletarianization" thesis put forward in 1994 within the confines of the anarchist Love & Rage organization. Day argued that the youth of the 1990s, because of the coming economic crisis, would be the first generation in the US to make less money than their parent generation and thus be in the first ranks of a reproletarianized working class. (See *www.spunk.org/texts/pubs/lr/sp001715/joelrept.html* for more information.)

5. When Lenin is referenced, which admittedly is quite rare, it is always a reference to *Left-Wing Communism: An Infantile Disorder*. Leaving aside the merits of this treatise, or

the quality of its interpretation, it is usually the case that those who cite *Left-Wing Communism* as justification for their neo-reformism are also the kinds of people who dislike most everything else that Lenin has written—so why do they treat him as an authority in this instance when they refuse to accept his authority in other issues? Because their interpretation of this treatise coincides with the politics they already espouse.

6. Indeed, both Mao Zedong and Carl Schmitt argued that a coherent political order begins by drawing a distinction between friends and enemies. To argue that this demonstrates a unity of thought between the radical communist and the nazi, however, is rather simplistic; all it demonstrates is that coherent political movements are able to grow in power by recognizing antagonistic and non-antagonistic relations—who to recruit, who not to recruit, who to oppose and isolate, who to support and reinforce. The similarity is only formal: a militant political order that wishes to come into being must understand who and what would oppose its emergence, the class basis of its ethics. The substantial differences beneath this formal similarity are more telling: the friend/enemy distinction of the fascist is precisely the distinction opposed by the communist and vice versa.

7. Biel, *The Entropy of Capitalism*, 6.

8. As it still is, and always has been, outside of the imperialist metropoles.

on the domestication of the left

"... with the revisionist/bourgeois union leaders having immersed the workers and employees in decades of economism and legalism, their hitting capacity has been temporarily stunted. And now, faced with an all-out offensive by the employers and the government they are, at present, ill-equipped to effectively fight back."

Anuradha Ghandy, Scripting the Change

1 Every political position that bypasses the norms established by the austerity apparatus to challenge the machine upon which it depends will be classified as totalitarian or "ultra-left." By whom? By either the apologists of the state of affairs or a traditional left leadership that has been domesticated by the social peace of welfare capitalism. In the end, the anxious subject of austerity, regardless of the direction it faces, wants the same thing: pacification.

If austerity is that which must be defeated at any cost (even if this cost implies that welfare capitalism can and should be "fixed") then a politics that does not collaborate with the terms imposed by its apparatus is guilty of foul play, of ruining the left for the more "rationally minded" activists and their sober understanding of socialism.

These totalitarians demanding a return to revolutionary communism, these "ultra-leftists" who speak of making the implicit civil war explicit, are possibly "destroying the chance of a real step in advance, and thereby delaying the whole movement" when they could be "supporting people whose ways are generally not [theirs], [and so] help the carrying out of such progressive measures" as the end of austerity. These words resonate now, especially amongst those austerity *socialist* subjects who like to (mis)quote Lenin's *Left-Wing Communism*, even though they belong to the 20th century's arch-renegade, the epitome of opportunism, Eduard Bernstein.[1] Again: the austerity apparatus and its subjective order might be novel but it is not new.

2 The political imagination atrophies, a neo-reformism becomes the limit of the real. When we are not arguing for a struggle aimed primarily at regrouping the left according to a new electoral movement that resembles Syriza, we are engaging in idle fantasies about Imaginary Parties, Invisible Committees, the autonomous multitude, etc. But even these fantasies are part of the same neo-reformist universe: they either function to prevent concrete practice, or are retained as a wishful delirium on the part of those whose regularized activism is reformist. To imagine anything else is heinous; the policing of the austerity apparatus enforces this belief—and why not? It has decades of anti-communist ideology informing its hegemony.

The austerity apparatus was assembled after, and according to, the capitalist end of history. It operates to ensure that this historical end remains a fact.

3 In opposition to the end of history that permitted the assemblage of the austerity apparatus there is that revolutionary politics that refuses to make reformism the primary focus of its operations and attempts to break with the order this apparatus works to normalize. But such a politics, being totalitarian and ultra-left, is forced to fight a theoretical people's war long before it can even imagine launching an actual people's war.

The moment it rears its defiant head communism is dismissed as heinous and unethical by the very people who claim fidelity to its history. Marxism "lacks an ethics" we are told, simply because it challenges the rules and philosophies of morality imposed by the bourgeois order, and so something else must be tried. Even self-proclaimed Marxists abide by this narrative when they complain about "Stalinism" and use the word totalitarian. The order of the ethical that is proclaimed by the austerity apparatus is all that matters: anything that attempts to violate business as usual is barbarism.

Thus even heroic attempts to reject the end of history are often assimilated by its discourse. Mark Fisher's *Capitalist Realism* was laudable in excavating the "realism" imposed by capitalism's end of history narrative; the extended essay attempts to critique "the widespread sense that not only is capitalism the only viable political and economic system, but also that it is now impossible even to *imagine* a coherent alternative."[2] Unfortunately Fisher capitulated to the terms of this capitalist realism: descriptions of economic "Stalinism" and "totalitarianism" are used uncritically, without any historical precision; he describes the state of the first world culture industry as if it is the experience of the world as a whole. Capitalist realism, the widespread attitude generated by the proclamation of the capitalist end of history, is endemic to the centres of capitalism; the subject who possesses this consciousness is not normative in the peripheries, nor are the cold war discursive concepts of "Stalinism" and "totalitarianism." If capitalist realism is the widespread sense that an alternative to capitalism is impossible, then part of this sense is to remain ignorant of those anti-capitalist revolutionary movements erupting in the global margins. Fisher is like a plague victim attempting to describe their own malaise: by speaking according to the terms of one's sickness a concrete diagnosis is impossible; all possible solutions are determined by the disease, the bare survival of a patient who can only think as a patient.

4 A particular discourse of democracy becomes the ethical terrain of the austerity apparatus and any politics that challenges this discourse is immediately discounted as immoral or lunatic. The right to vote in elections becomes the standard of morality: one is an ethical agent par excellence for simply practicing this right; another one is a total-itarian for challenging the way in which an individ-ual votes. People should have the right not to be shamed! Silencing is totalitarian! All politics that demand substance and mobilize the masses accord-ing to this substance are intimidating!

Here even the modern standard of liberal thought is abandoned: Mill's understanding of uni-versal suffrage, as elitist as it was, still maintained that liberal democracy was not defined by the oper-ation of electoral voting but by free debate. But now that "democracy" has been defined accord-ing to its electoral function, all that matters is the right to vote freely according to one's individual beliefs—and to hell with anyone who challenges an individual's beliefs no matter how anti-people these beliefs might be.

To be fair, this discourse is attempting to locate the concept of democracy according to the origi-nal meaning of the name. *Demos* never meant, as it is commonplace to assert, the popular masses—if this was the case, then it would make no sense for the ancient Athenians to coin this term in a context where the popular masses could *not* participate in politics: a patriarchal slave state. No, *demos* simply implied the district in which Athenian citizens were registered. The name *democracy* was originally understood as a government of the people who were recognized citizens. And though we might have different ideas about the concept of democracy now, isn't it also the case that in every state where democracy is invoked we discover a political order defined by the right of the recognized citizen? Not by the other, not by the oppressed masses, but by the rational bourgeois subject who assents to citizenship.

5 Homogenization according to democratic discourse becomes the norm for a left appropriated by the austerity apparatus. Even if a discourse of "difference" is utilized to undermine communist demands for class solidarity it is done so only to homogenize all of these differences into a common project of democratic damage control. Class struggle is collapsed according to a common anti-austerity agenda that all people, regardless of their class position, are expected to endorse. Those who reject this agenda and demand something more—something revolutionary—are accused of violating a rainbow coalition of liberalism.

Unity based on class solidarity is treated as a denial of difference, particularly different sites of oppression. Unity based on class collaboration, which is the cruelest form of homogenization, is first sublimated and then valorized.

The austerity subject is mistaken for a revolutionary subject when, in this case, the former is little more than a domesticated version of the latter—a diminishing echo across the chasm of decades: "revisionist contamination has completely tamed the so-called far left. Wild wolves who allow themselves to be trained become calm little dogs in just a few generations."[3]

6 An atavistic order, no matter how novel its mutation, always fears the agent that demands a revolutionary break. Hence the domestication of the potential revolutionary subject and a pseudo-truth procedure that operates so as to designate everything revolutionary, every break from the sameness of capitalism, as outmoded and old.

Capitalism's novelty is compelling; it can masquerade as always and ever *new*. New technologies, new eras, new conjunctures: nothing that is truly new, since it is all another version of the same old exploitation. But this procession of the real, now articulated (at the imperialist metropoles) by the austerity apparatus, is powerful enough to designate its opposite, the avatar of revolution, as something that belongs to a by-gone era.

With the end of history must come domestication, what Fisher partially examines as "capitalist realism," and the austerity apparatus is cunning enough to allow its subject to endorse its reality while being able to see right through it. Both the age of austerity and the revolutionary subject are rejected simultaneously; the redirection of rebellious energy is complete, a closed circuit. By rejecting the only way out of this strange loop as old-fashioned we find ourselves thrown back to its point of origin.

7 Breaking from bourgeois legality is horrific according to the subject domesticated by austerity. All forms of anti-capitalist militancy become suspect for the most domesticated subject; individualized and incoherent militancy become de facto for the less domesticated subject. And yet the same domestication is often demonstrated by those who reject the domestication of militant practice; the proliferation of liberal ideology is not easily escaped.

Both the neo-reformist "socialist" and the Black Bloc activist are united in their domestication, despite their hatred for one another. Both develop narratives that explain how and why their rivals are cops; both are suspicious of a coherent revolutionary subject assembled by a partisan war machine—a comprehensive and fighting revolutionary party.

Even still, the domestication of the neo-reformist is more complete, particularly since it seeks to quell the militancy of its counterpart, to bring it in line with a "realistic" vision of socialism. And when it fails to discipline the excessive behaviour of its other, it dismisses such behaviour as ultra-leftism and engages in conspiracy theories about agent provocateur activities. While it is correct to recognize that the state machinery may often engage in violent provocations, it is far more correct to realize that this same machinery relies to a greater degree on the most domesticated factions of the left policing its more radical members so as to ensure social peace.

8 A domesticated left that collaborates in the promotion of a state of social peace in the name of socialism is nothing new. There is a long history of buying off entire sections of the left and the working-class leadership: not necessarily through conspiratorial back-room deals and literal exchanges of money (which might occasionally happen just as violent agents provocateurs are occasionally used) but through a structural system of management.

For example, the labour aristocracy is not an existent strata because of a deal struck at some historical moment between factions of the working class and capital, but because of the processes that resulted from the historic compromise between capital and labour. This example demonstrates that structural changes in the internal functioning of capital produce reasons for a specific portion of the class to develop a consciousness that is contrary to the class as a whole. And the left in general is not beyond this structural shift: instituted leaderships, state-funding for would-be radical organizations, and the fact that the ideology of the ruling class is a common sense norm mean that broad sections of the left has, can, and will be brought into line with the daily operations of capital.

Why is it easier for the bureaucracy of a national trade union—and often the Executive and

Bargaining Team bodies of a local—to cooperate with the supposed necessity of social peace than it is for the rank-and-file? Why will this rank-and-file, though sometimes more radical than its leadership, accept the economistic limits of legal unionism? Why is it that the popularity of some left wing organizations relies on receiving money from either state-owned institutions or structures that themselves receive such funding? What consciousness, what behaviour, does this promote? Domestication.

Under the austerity apparatus, however, the novelty of this domestication is that it is embraced while, at the same time, accepted as fact. The austerity subject can quote from books and articles that recognize why "the revolution will not be funded" but simultaneously remain addicted to this funding. According to the age of austerity this is the best we can get.

9 The domestication promoted by the austerity apparatus is alien to the lowest strata of the proletariat. The working poor, whose life was already austere, are rarely convinced that they need to "tighten their belts" and abide by the austerity ideology when there are no belts left to tighten. In many ways the contradictions of capitalism are apparent to this down-and-out faction of workers. Here domestication operates according to older principles: a proliferation of religious mystification and conspiracy theories.

The type of domestication generated by the austerity apparatus is aimed primarily at the petty-bourgeoisie, particularly that section of the petty-bourgeoisie that is being reproletarianized. It is a containment policy, class inoculation.

10 We use the term domestication intentionally; the point is to set ourselves apart from those analyses that attempt to identify self-policing with policing itself. Simply because we police ourselves according to ruling class ideology—that we assent to ideological discipline because we have been socialized according to capitalist norms—does not mean that there is no longer a distinction between the citizens and the police of a given state of affairs. The collapsing of this distinction is something that Althusser, despite his problems, critiqued decades ago when he mocked the anarchist notion of an "inner cop" in the mind of the well-intentioned activist.

The actual police and the citizens engaged in self-policing are still distinct categories, separated by entire worlds. The latter is a result of machinations that are primarily ideological; the former, though still plugged into dominant ideology, is part of a concrete state apparatus: a legal entity, an actual institution of armed bodies who possess a much more coherent function than any subject that assents to this function.

Ruling class ideology indeed operates as a mirror for the values of the ruled, but simply because we are socialized to accept capitalist values as common sense does not mean that we are all capitalists: the entire social universe that is captivated by capital is not completely comprised of literal capitalists. Simply because someone accepts the capitalist order is not enough to make them an actual capitalist, an owner of the means of production. Similarly, simply because one polices their behaviour—and perhaps even polices others according to the state of social peace—does not make them an actual cop.

The concrete distinction is very easy to grasp. The average citizen, no matter how domesticated, does not possess the same social power as the cop. Outside of literal policing institutions they are not empowered to make arrests, carry and use weapons with the same impunity, engage with the legal apparatus in the same manner. These are significant boundaries that produce social meaning, codified by uniforms and badges.

It is the austerity apparatus that seeks to collapse these distinctions, to make us believe that the citizen is the same as the police officer and vice versa. The message is clear: there is no escape from the discipline of capital.

11 To be accurate, domestication through the austerity apparatus is the result of a long process, the consummation of what originated with the imperialist belle époque in the metropoles. The historic concession between labour and capital, the emergence of welfare capitalism, is the origin point: the crystallization of the culture industry and its delirium of repressive desublimation is the genesis of domestication. In order to domesticate a subject there need to be material reasons for this domestication, a discipline that does not produce rebellion: imperialism provided the means with which to buy-out large sections of the masses, swelling the ranks of the so-called "middle class," and produce a culture industry in which domestication was accompanied with certain privileges.

After decades of welfare capitalism, however, the next crisis cannot be denied. Moreover, with a population already domesticated by the material basis of the culture industry it became possible to delink the culture industry from the welfare capitalism upon which it depended. The crisis that began in 2008 was, by all reports, worse than the Great Depression, but the culture industry's delirium made it difficult for us to realize this was the case even when it was destroying our place at the kid's table of the master's banquet. Mainstream media reported only spectacle, even in the midst of reporting the crisis's excesses, so that one could be poor and still think they lived in the best country on the face of the planet—that whatever woes they experienced were just a hiccup, the result of their own poor choices, and not a common experience shared by many. In the midst of tent cities and itinerant homeless populations we were given more Transformers movies, silly talk shows, and celebrity gossip.

The narrative of the "disappearing middle class" was part of the austerity apparatus's discursive operation. Reproletarianization is a threat to the ruling class: capitalists don't want the victims of the crisis to recognize that they might be becoming part of the working masses—which was what they would have been before the historic concession between labour and capital, which is what they always kind of were but as an *elite*—and so it became ideologically necessary to promote a consciousness of a class that was never really an actual class. A vague "middle class" that only existed in the first place because of imperialist privilege that the crisis was slowly eroding. But after decades of being part of this pseudo-class, after subordination to the culture industry, the austerity subject has learned to accept its domestication.

The domestication of austerity, then, is a second order domestication: a domestication of the already domesticated. The novelty of this domestication, however, is this: where we were once domesticated because of privilege, we are now being domesticated to accept the end of this privilege. That is, our domestication is such that we either demand a return to the previous era of domestication or just accept, heads meekly bowed, that we must prepare ourselves for a brutal austerity armageddon.

12 Now ill-equipped to deal with austerity, the traditional leadership of the left and working class finds itself outmaneuvered. Austerity reigns, domestication is complete, reproletarianization is denied by campaigns of collaboration. And yet the fact remains that reproletarianization is happening and only decades of economistic privilege amongst the ranks of the crumbling labour aristocracy and its culture industry are keeping the masses in line.

Between capital and the most oppressed masses of the imperialist metropoles the bulwark of a domesticated leadership is becoming paper thin. Reproletarianization of the so-called "middle classes" means also the regeneration of the lowest levels of the working class, the formation of a proletarian hard core that is slipping the yoke of its domesticated leadership. This is a class that was never as integrated, that is becoming less and less enamoured with those who speak in its name, and that develops in the cracks of welfare capitalism—opened by the austerity apparatus—because it has been long excluded from the unions and labour councils, ignored by a left that focused only on those workers already organized by capital.

Along with the domesticated austerity subject we also discover the germ of its hated double: the revolutionary subject, the very thing the austerity apparatus forbids.

notes

1. The concluding paragraph of *Karl Marx and Social Reform,* an essay that argued that Marx's theory of class struggle was best understood through the lens of social reform. This essay, along with other works by Bernstein, prompted Rosa Luxemburg to write her classic rejoinder, *Social Reform or Revolution?,* that relegated Bernstein to the dustbin of history. Unfortunately, the ideas he espoused are always popular amongst that faction of the left that want to collaborate with capitalism while maintaining a socialist veneer.

2. Mark Fisher, *Capitalist Realism: Is There No Alternative?* (Winchester: Zero Books, 2009), 2.

3. PCR-RCP, "Legitimate Revolt is not a Conspiracy" (www.pcr-rcp.ca/en/archives/1045).

a partisan war machine and its counter-state

"... forms-of-life confront one another as partisan war machines."

Tiqqun, *Introduction to Civil War*

1 Although the austerity apparatus functions to forbid the emergence of a revolutionary subject—to channel all rebellious energy towards a collaboration with the state of social peace—this subject is necessitated by the fact of reproletarianization. Harsher operations of capitalism mean that workers will become conscious of these operations, particularly if they occupied the lowest ranks of the working class before the policies of austerity were conceived.

The austerity apparatus, however, functions so as to contain these rebellious subjects, to pull them back into its operations. Its anxious subjects—either would-be fascists or domesticated opportunists—are deployed as agents of containment.

2 Just as the state of affairs instinctively, according to its day-to-day operations, develops various apparatuses in order to produce domesticated subjects, so too should any movement that aims to be a counter-state develop similar apparatuses. Earlier we claimed that what now goes by the name "austerity" in some ways represents capitalism's ultimate horizon—its internal and pitiless crisis logic rendered bare—while simultaneously communism represents capitalism's altimate (that is, an alter-ultimate) horizon. In order to conceptualize this other horizon, and how it must be approached concretely (rather than proposed in an abstract manner), we must think of it as a counter-state of affairs that needs to be brought into being by producing its own subjects, institutions, culture, and ideology.

3 A counter-state of affairs cannot be brought into being spontaneously, or by the assumption that multiple sites of struggle lacking organizational unity constitute a coherent movement. The proliferation of struggles against the state of affairs is indeed a healthy multiplicity when compared to the entropy of capitalist singularity; but its inability, by itself, to demonstrate a counter-singularity (that is, a counter-state of affairs capable of building its own alter-hegemonic apparatuses) is also its weakness.

What is required is a comprehensive, fighting revolutionary party. A *partisan war machine*.

4 While it is indeed the case that capitalism is a failing machine, an assemblage cobbled together by cannibalized parts, the partisan war machine signals a new assemblage that will be like capitalism as a modern computer is to a word processor. Perhaps an organic analogy would be more appropriate, but this would simply reify a distinction between the natural and artificial that privileges the former. Cancer is also organic and capitalism has reached its cancerous stage.

There is nothing wrong with assuming that there are better machines rather than, conversely, opposing the organic to the machinic. We already know that some machines are better than others, just as we know that the accelerationists are half-ways correct when they privilege utopian forces of production. Lenin privileged one assemblage of state machinery over another; Mao talked about taking up the gun to get rid of the gun. The partisan war machine will necessarily wither away when it has achieved its aims; if it persists, becoming static and outdated, then its machinery should be challenged.

Moreover, the analogy of "war machine" has already been given an organic designation by Deleuze and Guattari, defined as rhizomatic when divested of partisan hegemony and diffused according to a nomadic ethos. The war machine "seems to be irreducible to the State apparatus, to be outside its sovereignty and prior to its law; it comes from elsewhere."[1] A war machine is an assemblage developed in the interest of waging war, directing all of its multiple functions and parts towards a singular purpose. In the case of a *revolutionary* war machine, this purpose is the consummation of class war against capitalist hegemony. Hence, such war machines "take shape against the apparatuses that appropriate the machine and make war their affair and their object: they bring connections to bear against the great conjunction of the apparatuses of capture and domination."[2]

But such a war machine must be guided by a coherent *partisan* perspective: it must be practically and theoretically organized. Without this perspective, a combative counter-hegemony will lapse into movementist spontaneity, an incoherence that has done little more but embrace the so-called "end of history."

5 The partisan war machine, the revolutionary party that intervenes from a position of unified singularity, is necessary because a political class that is conscious of itself as a class cannot otherwise exist. As Lazzarato explains, in an attempt to excavate the reality imposed by austerity capitalism at the imperialist metropoles:

> No longer based in the factory, the new class composition that has emerged over the years is made up of a multiplicity of situations of employment, non-employment, occasional employment, and greater or lesser poverty. It is dispersed, fragmented, and precarious, far from finding the means to constitute a political "class" even if it represents the majority of the population.[3]

Unfortunately he takes this fact of dispersal and fragmentation as evidence that the proletariat no longer exists as a potential political subject, subordinated as it is to the subjectivation mobilized by crisis capitalism. Worse, he loses himself in the unsubstantiated claim that the class struggle is between debtor and capital rather than labour and capital. As is typical of these chic theoretical operations, the solution is a non-solution: "[l]azy action… the exact opposite of the purpose-driven action of capitalist production."[4] A refusal to do anything but refuse, because there is no class composition beyond the molecular; dispersal into vague categories of debtor and creditor must mean a dropping out of organizing altogether with the pretense that such a refusal is synonymous with organization.

What Lazzarato should have grasped is that the revolutionary class can never constitute itself as a political class without the intervention of a party. Even before this fragmentation, when the first world proletariat *was* discovered within the organized industrial factories, it was still unable to constitute itself as a political class, to be the proletariat *for itself*. Why? Because trade union consciousness was the norm, an earlier form of economism dominated, and the limits were established by bourgeois ideology. He skirts this understanding so as to declare, in a stunning refusal to examine the literature, that "[n]o less than the rest of the Marxist tradition, Lenin fails to foresee the integration of the working class and the population into the capitalist economy through increases in wage and income."[5]   Stunningly, he manages to undermine this claim several pages later when he articulates the very theory (e.g. "the labour aristocracy") that Lenin put forward to account for the very thing he supposedly failed to explain.[6] The point being, this integration *was* foreseen and theorized. Following

Lenin, there is an already existent theorization of the integration and dispersal of the working class.

Although today's partisan war machine must locate its subject in this dispersal, rather than hoping to discover it waiting in unionized sites of production, the task remains the same: organize those who have nothing left to lose but their chains around a revolutionary project; go deeper into the masses; establish a fighting, political class.

6 The current capitalist state of affairs is strong precisely because of its ability to link all of the multiplicities of ruling class dominance to the singularity of capitalist logic. Having long since passed the point of taking power—having succeeded in making the transition to capitalism—the ruling class has completed its hegemony. It can set aside its earlier forms of singularity where partisan war machines of the capitalist type were required in order to wage an organized war against various tributary social formations. The English Civil War had its partisan war machine. So too did the French Revolution. Other examples abound. In order to bring its counter-state into existence, the ascendant bourgeois order required its version of comprehensive, fighting revolutionary parties—innumerable would-be and actual avant garde parties—that existed to establish the hegemony of an emergent class order over centuries of attempted transitions.

The partisan war machine is discarded when class hegemony is achieved and, with the ideological order of this class (including all of its discursive operations) established as a fact of nature and the mirror of values, an order of political electoral parties can be established. That is, a conjuncture is reached in which, upon achieving hegemony, the partisan war machine can be deployed amongst multiple civil parties while remaining immanent to all of them. Hence, under capitalism, all electoral parties are variants of the same partisan war machine, a multiplicity conditioned by the singularity of capital, even when they call themselves socialist. These are not parties that produce partisan subjects interested in waging war upon the ruling class; as part of the state of affairs they can only produce subjects that are partisan, in different ways, to the bourgeois order. Beneath all of this the immanent partisan war machine continues to produce apparatuses—with discourses and subjectivities—that reinforce its class order.

7 A partisan war machine provides the kind of singularity to class struggle that is necessary to break the limits imposed by the current state of affairs. The name "austerity" now defines these limits; as long as we accept the narrative of the austerity apparatus we will also accept these limits. We require a machine with operations designed to lay siege to these limits with apparatuses that will function as siege engines, subjects who will function as soldiers.

To conceptualize such a war machine as already being diffuse, vaguely deployed amongst a nebulous movement that is believed to be the magical result of disconnected and multiple sites of struggle, is to imagine that we have already achieved the kind of hegemony where this diffusion is possible. Hence, every theory of micro-politics, autonomous workerism, Imaginary Parties and Invisible Committees, and anarchist desaturation fails to grasp the significance of partisan singularity.

If capitalism can tolerate a certain level of multiplicity—different capitalist parties with conflicting values—this is only because it already imposed its singular hegemony. It already utilized explicit fighting parties, in different regions where it began to establish its class rule, so as to force a state of affairs that would make its promised mode of production universal. Of course it is this underlying singularity—the singularity of capital—that fears the multiplicity of the masses, the confusion of rebellion, the angry hordes at the doorstep of the corn-dealer.[7]

Against this we need another singular politics that, in its singularity, can mobilize the mass multiplicity that the current singular order fears. To the singularity of the bourgeoisie we raise the singularity of the proletariat. Against the multiple variants of the bourgeois order we must raise the multiple sites of rebellion that this order attempts to contain.

8 The revolutionary partisan war machine will produce its own subjects; such subjects do not exist, in a complete form, outside of this comprehensive fighting party. What we find instead are partial subjects primed for mobilization, those whose being and consciousness are defined by resistance to the bourgeois order, who are not easily domesticated or managed by the austerity apparatus. The most rebellious faction of these potential subjects exists at the lowest level of the state of affairs, the so-called "hard core of the proletariat." Those who already understand that they have nothing left to lose but their chains, who instinctively desire to become revolutionary subjects.

Even still, the revolutionary subject does not fully exist prior to a revolutionary party that is capable of pulling it into its orbit. Here there is only a fragmented and potential existence, a rebellious dream of an operationalized subject—a conflicted subject, a manner of being that instinctively resists the subjectivity capitalism works to impose. Only the singularity of a partisan war machine will functionalize these possible subjects, providing the necessary movement unity.

9 Is there a problem of origins? How can this partisan war machine come into existence without a prior subject? That is, if such a movement is responsible for producing subjects then how can it even exist if there is no subject capable of establishing its existence? If the machine produces the subject then its existence prior to the subject becomes a problem: there would be nothing capable of making it revolutionary in the first place, social structures do not simply pop into existence without human interaction.

But the subjection to the bourgeois order is not complete—the bourgeois subject has always contained it opposite—and a history of this revolutionary other has been in effect since the origin of capitalism. Hence an incomplete counter-subject already exists: enough to compose the basic framework of a partisan war machine but not enough to make this framework singular. The revolutionary singularity is a process, becoming emergent through a variety of historical experiences, figuring out its subjectivity in every situation. A subject in process, a subject that must always find ways to connect its organized party to the rebellious masses so as to develop this subject further.

The subject of the First International was culled from the experience of the counter-subjectivity of early capitalism. The Second International was an attempt to force the rebellious proletarian subject back into the bourgeois order. The subject of the Third International, rejecting the Second, was developed through the experience of a vast revolutionary experience. The subject of the anti-revisionist movement, launched by the Chinese Revolution, was a subject patched together by experiences of rebellion within the socialist transition. At this conjuncture, we have a theory of the subject from which to begin. Not complete, weaker than the subject promised by the bourgeois order, but a subject that exists within the cracks of the state of affairs just as an incomplete bourgeois subject existed within the cracks of the tributary state of affairs.

10 "Resistance" is treated as a dirty word in some quarters. The accelerationists, for example, believe we need to abandon terms of conflict; they implicitly endorse social peace with the austerity apparatus. Lazzarato attempts to substitute resistance and organized struggle with the categories of refusal and laziness. Resistance, rebellion, revolution, armed struggle, class war—outmoded concepts, according to some thinkers and movements that brand themselves radical. More antiquated than liberalism, apparently, because this is what is implied by the rejection of combative politics that dare to draw clear lines of demarcation: an endorsement of liberalism as the most radical position possible, an acceptance of a peaceful transition to post-capitalism, a refusal to challenge the very apparatus that interpellates our subjectivity.

Establishment terror of the revolutionary agent is reanimated according to the novelty of the austerity apparatus. Now it is properly "radical" to dismiss any form of resistance that is not contained by the state of affairs. We no longer need the aegis of the cold war or the red scare to contain rebel ideology: quarantine is possible through a discourse that appeals to a history of radical language in order to enforce the state of affairs.

11 The subject mobilized by the austerity apparatus cannot tolerate a renegade partisan war machine. Since the austerity apparatus functions to defend the state of affairs of which it is a part—and since this state of affairs exists to defend a particular mode of production (and was the result of the bourgeois partisan war machine that established this mode of production)—its subject order will necessarily be hostile to anything that operates to establish a counter-state of affairs, and thus a new mode of production. Even when the austerity subject veils itself as "left" it remains hostile to anything that begins to resemble a comprehensive, fighting, and revolutionary party of the exploited and oppressed classes.

Anxiety becomes pronounced when we encounter a singular and revolutionary order that makes us question the limits of rebellion we have been socialized to believe are correct. Never mind the fact that these limits are limits imposed by capital, or that our anxiety about the transgression of business as usual is inherent to austerity's subjecthood. We are bothered by the spectre of a singular partisan war machine: we pretend that it is antiquated; cold warrior narratives about totalitarianism are mobilized.

Sometimes, upon realizing its necessity, we attempt to banish the revolutionary party to the shadows of our anxious activity. If we must accept its importance then we pretend that it will emerge spontaneously and argue that it ought not be confused with what its existence necessarily requires. Better the vague promise of such a machine than one that is concretely assembled according to a coherent class politics; better the machine that builds itself, the complex mechanism that is also its own cause.

12 Revolutionary partisan war machines do not will themselves into existence—they do not spontaneously manifest, like djinn freed from the magic bottles of a multitude of struggles—but are consciously constructed through struggle. There will be failed machines, competing blueprints, parties that end up being captured by the state apparatus and reintegrated in the capitalist order, anachronistic inventions that keep functioning despite the fact that they do nothing except chug along as antiquated curiousities. Most machines successful in solving a particular problem were not the only proposed solution.

Faced with the potential eruption of multiple partisan constructions, and aware that many of these will either fail or become relegated to activist obscurity, the (left) subject of the austerity apparatus often reacts with antipathy. Failure and confusion only confirm anxiety; it is better, this subject reasons, to pursue a neo-reformist politics and refuse to recognize that this channeling of energy is precisely what produces its anxiety. Even worse, like an addict that recognizes the anxiety they experience between fixes is the result of the fix itself, there are austerity subjects who recognize the problems of their political practice *but would still rather pursue this practice* than involve themselves with a revolutionary partisan political order. It's hard to kick a bad habit.

13 Elsewhere we spoke of a "new return" to the concept of the theoretically and practically unified revolutionary party.[8] Elsewhere we argued that this new return was best signified by the partisan project promised by Marxism-Leninism-Maoism.[9] But what does this new return mean, practically, in the face of the austerity apparatus that unceasingly operates to enforce the singular order of capitalism? How can a counter-order, with the same unflinching singularity, unfold in a landscape where multiple rebellions have been attenuated, undermined, appropriated?

One solution to this problem would be to propose the kind of partisan war machine that belongs in 1917, or even 1948, where these multiple sites of rebellion had not yet produced their own historical trajectories. There was no consolidated feminist movement, anti-racist movement, queer movement, etc. in these periods, though the revolutionary orders at those times possessed the potential to incorporate them in their civil wars. We find subterranean histories of this potential, an entire and conflicted body of theory that demonstrates these problematics were not ignored by some stereotypical understanding of class struggle in the abstract. Unfortunately, those who seek an old return to the problem of the party ignore these subterranean histories of their own movement and reduce everything to the vaguest and most abstract understanding of class struggle, transforming events such as the October Revolution into moribund caricatures.

Today's partisan war machine cannot afford a return to such an unqualified singularity. Rather, its revolutionary totality must mobilize and systematize multiple sites of rebellion, transforming them into coherent apparatuses and directed operations. These rebellious sites cannot be ignored in the hope that they will be solved by some bland and unqualified notion of class struggle; they need to be linked and subordinated to this machine's over-arching struggle, made coherent by its singularity. After all, most struggles against exploitation and capitalism, despite whatever limitations they possess, in some ways demonstrate important insights about class struggle as a whole—they can educate and transform any potential coherent movement.

14 Today's partisan war machine must be a movement of movements, a singular complex of repurposed multiplicities. A class struggle machine that, under its aegis, collects and assembles feminist, anti-racist, Indigenous, queer, anti-ableist, trans, and numerous other anti-systemic struggles that, by themselves, are incapable of challenging the state of affairs. A proliferation of mass organizations and fronts that are transformed by a singular civil war machine—a revolutionary party that draws in these disconnected movements—but also transform this machine into something that is more than the sum of its parts.

When a singular revolutionary movement contains entire movements there is a point where the quantitative becomes the qualitative. By mobilizing all of these rebellious movements under a coherent party structure, there is the point where the machine becomes more significant than what number of movements it has been able to draw into its operations. Here begins a qualitative shift in the machine itself, where this quantity of very particular components revalorize its development. Here begins the partisan war machine that is not merely assembling internal movements but is being repurposed as a class struggle movement based on the trajectories it has chosen to encode with its own dominant trajectory, a trajectory aimed at the dissolution of capitalism.

notes

1. Deleuze and Guattari, *A Thousand Plateaus* (Minneapolis: University of Minnesota Press, 1998), 352.

2. Ibid., 423.

3. Maurizio Lazzarato, *Governing by Debt* (South Pasadena, Semiotext[e], 2015), 12–13.

4. Ibid., 252.

5. Ibid., 230.

6. Ibid., 234–235.

7. As noted in a previous section, Mill's fear of the chaos of rebellion is defined in that telling passage of *On Liberty* where he limits free expression to the marketplace of ideas, claiming that a disorganized mob assembled at the home of a corn-dealer engaged in starving this mob constitute a violation of liberty. Freedom in words but not in actions, the latter of which would viscerally challenge bourgeois hegemony. Obey punctually; censor freely. The fact that the state of affairs described by Mill was only possible because of violent challenges to pre-bourgeois hegemony is left out of the equation. By this time capitalism's partisan war machines have done their work: Mill was merely describing the rules of an already established game. Moreover, it is worth noting just how institutionalized these rules have become since, how the political position inherent in the corn-dealer example has become common-sense. It is not uncommon for progressives, even those who call themselves "Marxist," to define any unruly attack on business-as-usual—that is, anything that violates the rules of liberal good behaviour—as heinous, often using the word "fascist" (despite the fact that this term would have been alien to Mill) to describe

situations that precisely resemble the unruly masses gathered outside of the corn-dealer's home.

8. In *The Communist Necessity* (Montreal: Kersplebedeb, 2014).

9. In *Continuity and Rupture* (Winchester: Zero Books, 2016).

afterword

To apprehend austerity as a discursive apparatus of
capitalism's most recent crisis is to grasp the process it attempts to conceal: the reproletarianization
of the working classes in the imperialist metropoles.
Such a process is precisely why the austerity subject
has been constructed, why we have been taught that
the partisan war machine is antiquated, and why
the civil war has been sublimated according to the
reified order of an anxious state of affairs.

The immanent threat of a state of emergency
(increased surveillance, the criminalization of dissent, an even broader definition of "terrorism")
is part of this so-called age of austerity. A leaner
economic reality, where all social programs are
annihilated, demands a meaner security apparatus:
brutal police measures, explicit social control. And
yet these obvious forms of coercion are becoming
less and less shocking due to the over-realization
of bourgeois hegemony. There was a time when

the bourgeoisie was forced to use explicit coercion in order to establish a state of affairs in which it was hegemonic—where it could rule by a primarily non-coercive consent, resorting only to coercion when it was faced with the resistance of its most marginalized populations. Now its hegemony has reached the point that everyone is consenting to coercion itself, where the state of affairs can openly repress anyone and everywhere with a large measure of impunity.

These are, after all, *austere times*. And faced with this reality why would we not desire a return to that kinder and gentler capitalism? On the one hand the austerity apparatus functions to produce these austere times, on the other hand it functions to redirect its more rebellious subjects into a struggle against the apparatus rather than against the machine of which it is a part.

Since the austerity apparatus is an attempt to jury-rig a capitalism that transgressed its limits long ago, entering the realm of moribund parasitism, it also functions to conceal what Biel defines as the system's implicit entropy:

> We now enter a phase marked by chaotic features, not just environmentally, but because the capitalist mode of production which organized humanity over a long period is losing its grip. Since disorder

is there anyway, why not embrace it as an opportunity for change? The ruling system can still meet
this challenge by playing a double game, posing as
guarantor of order while actually promoting those
chaotic features which stimulate a security reflex.
The problem is, though, that it cannot even master
its *own* chaotic features by creating a stable, new
accumulation regime: it lacks new institutional
ideas or fresh energy sources of a kind which
fuelled past efforts of regime-building[1]

On the one hand the state of anxiety, on the
other hand the state of emergency. The promise
of a state of social peace can only be partial; the
complete restabilization of welfare capitalism is a
never realized delirium that will still appropriate
the energy of would-be leftists. Despite entropy,
and because of this promised delirium, the austerity apparatus will find ways to channel its subjects
into activities that patch over the holes of a capitalism coming apart, "thus harnessing [otherwise
subversive] energies in a non-threatening manner,
notably to offset the social entropy caused through
pauperization. Hence the 'sustainable communities'
discourse."[2]

The fact that there can be no sustainable communities within the boundaries drawn by capitalism is enough to produce a state of anxiety: we

realize this is the case but, despite this realization, anxiously attempt to sustain the state of affairs by demanding an end of austerity rather than an end of capitalism.

At the same time, however, the state of affairs is not such that, as Lazzarato claims, "capitalism has completely shifted to the very 'abstract' and 'deterritorialized' ground of debt."[3] The debt economy is not the ground of contemporary capitalism; it is merely one novel characteristic amongst many: the creditor-debtor contradiction, after all, would not be possible without a global apparatus of labour, that is still primarily *industrial*, that has signified the order of the real in contradiction to the speculative/fictitious order of the imaginary—these aspects of capitalism, when combined, were behind the recent crisis. Fictitious capitalism, the so-called *dematerialization* of capital, found itself at odds with the concrete fact of production; the ground remained the contradiction between capital and labour—one cannot speculate and accumulate profits for very long without the labour that produces this surplus-value in the first place. Capitalism still remains more than a debt economy, though it does employ the strategy of debt in this age of austerity.

Indeed, to focus primarily on the debt economy may be a stratagem ordained by the austerity apparatus. "We must fight for the cancellation of debt," Lazzarato argues, "for debt, one will recall, is not an economic problem but an apparatus of power designed not only to impoverish us, but to bring about catastrophe."[4] At best, this is a partial truth: while it is the case that debt "is not an economic problem but an apparatus of power," to focus our militant energy on the cancellation of debt is precisely what the austerity apparatus will permit because this is yet another struggle against austerity rather than capitalism itself. As discussed, "the indebted man" is a subject position that is *not* a political class—this is the point.

Capitalism can survive without its current debt economy, although due to its current addiction to this aspect of its economy it might end up moving towards a particular state of emergency—a tendency Biel has called *exterminism*. Anti-austerity movements are premised on the fight for the cancellation of debt, amongst other things, but this does not make them anti-capitalist. Syriza, for example, came into power based on a program of debt cancellation rather than a program of seizing socialist power, and this was the focus of its fight and we now understand where this has led: not to the end of capitalism, not to socialism, not to a fight that can even be pursued without first pursuing a struggle that comprehends the primary social contradiction: capital-labour, bourgeois-proletariat. If we wish to abolish debt then we need to abolish this fundamental social contradiction.

To reject austerity is not to be contained by its apparatus where our energy is channeled into a limited rejection of neoliberal reforms. Austerity will only be rejected when capitalism is overthrown. Only a partisan war machine that "comes from outside"—is built outside of the logic that capitalism claims is reality itself—is capable of laying siege to the austere fortifications of today's state of affairs.

notes

1. Biel, *The Entropy of Capitalism*, 14.

2. Ibid., 16.

3. Lazzarato, *The Making of the Indebted Man*, 161.

4. Ibid., 164.

Acknowledgments

This was a fun book to make in the wake of *Continuity and Rupture* and I should begin by thanking K at Kersplebedeb, who first took a chance on me with *The Communist Necessity*, for deciding that this was a worthwhile project to pursue. Since I was a big fan of their catalogue from before they put out my first book, it's great to remain part of the roster. I treasure all of our discussions.

Next I need to acknowledge the editing work done by both my partner, Vicky Moufawad-Paul, and my close friend Jude Welburne. My relationship with Jude goes back to the first year of my doctorate and every political position I have claimed over the years has benefited from his insightful engagement. He has always challenged my thought in a supportive and honest manner. I can't wait until his Marxist work on Milton, More, and utopian literature receives the attention it deserves.

I'm also supremely grateful to the two individuals, Colleen Bell and Benjanun Sriduangkaew, who agreed to read and then endorse this book many months in advance of its publication.

Colleen is a long time friend and colleague and her work on the Canadian security apparatus remains some of the best critical left literature on the development of Canada's repressive state apparatus post-9/11. We go way back to the days when we organized together, along with her partner Jesse, in the same union local. She is one of the few colleagues from that period and circle of friends who succeeded in getting tenure which, due to the small number of such jobs these days, speaks to her brilliance and tenacity as an academic. The fact that this job has taken her out west and away from us is especially bittersweet since my daughter Samiya enjoyed playing with her son Noah. I'm glad we have been able to maintain our friendship, I look forward to her visits, and I hope that we can find ways to keep our children close as they grow up.

Benjanun's endorsement of this book is some-thing I find quite exciting. Before contacting her with the request I was a devoted fan of her fiction. Indeed, when I first thought of asking her to read and blurb the book (a possibly heterodox decision because often the fiction and non-fiction worlds are kept separate) I delayed out of an anxiety generated by my love of her work. I was surprised when she agreed to read the draft and more surprised when she decided to endorse it. Since then I've enjoyed her twitter friendship. For those readers who are unfamiliar with her, Benjanun writes the greatest SFF short stories I've read since Ballard, with the prose skill of an Angela Carter. Since she's been nominated for many of the coveted SFF awards it's only a matter of time before she wins one. She also has an award-nominated novella, *Scale-Bright*. Within her writing context she has been an unrelenting critic of the state of affairs, so much so that she has experienced the typical shitty backlash from pseudo-left liberals. The fact that she continues publishing excellent work in the face of GamerGate-style harrassment is awe-inspiring and demands our support.

I would also like to acknowledge and commemorate Nathalie Moreau who will never have a chance to read this book and provide me with encouragement and/or criticism. Indeed, when I started to prepare the manuscript of *Austerity Apparatus* for publication, right at the time when *Continuity and Rupture*, which was partly dedicated to her, was about to be released, Nathalie passed away after a long fight with ovarian cancer. Nathalie was a tireless organizer for the PCR-RCP, one of its founding ideologues, and a significant portion of my theoretical understanding is indebted to her infuence... Or, rather, the influence of "Gabrielle" which was the organizational name those of us involved in groups that supported the PCR-RCP knew her by—the name used in the dedication in *Continuity and Rupture*. Her death is a loss but her legacy is an inspiration: she inspired and recruited a generation of Canadian revolutionaries; she continued organizing with her comrades right up until three weeks before her death. Now I have to imagine what she would think of this more heterodox publication, though I suspect she would have enjoyed it.

Finally, I would like to thank my parents who have encouraged me to think and write from a young age and probably should have been thanked/acknowledged in previous books. Although they have occasionally been bemused by the direction of my politics and the content of my books, they have always been supportive.

About the Author

J. Moufawad-Paul lives in Toronto with his partner, artist and curator Vicky Moufawad-Paul, and their daughter Samiya. He works as adjunct faculty at York University where he received his doctorate in Philosophy. He is the author of *The Communist Necessity* and *Continuity and Rupture,* and he blogs at the popular *MLM Mayhem.*

Kersplebedeb Publishing

ALL POWER TO THE PEOPLE
ALBERT "NUH" WASHINGTON

1894820215 • 111 pp. • $10.00

A collection of writings by the late Albert Nuh Washington, a former member of the Black Panther Party and Black Liberation Army. Washington was imprisoned in 1971 as a result of the U.S. government's war against the Black Liberation Movement. (2002)

AMAZON NATION OR ARYAN NATION: WHITE WOMEN AND THE COMING OF BLACK GENOCIDE
BOTTOMFISH BLUES

9781894946551 • 160 pp. • $12.95

The massive New Afrikan uprisings of the 1960s were answered by the white ruling class with the destruction of New Afrikan communities coast to coast, the decimation of the New Afrikan working class, the rise of the prison state and an explosion of violence between oppressed people. Taken on their own, in isolation, these blights may seem to be just more "social issues" for NGOs to get grants for, but taken together and in the context of amerikkkan history, they constitute genocide. (2014)

BASIC POLITICS OF MOVEMENT SECURITY
J. SAKAI & MANDY HISCOCKS

9781894946520 • 68 pp. • $7.00

Introducing issues regarding movement security, and the political ramifications thereof. A transcript of a talk Sakai gave at the Montreal Anarchist Bookfair in 2013, and an interview with Hiscocks about how her political scene and groups she worked with were infiltrated by undercover agents a year before the 2010 G20 summit in Toronto. (2014)

CATEGORIES OF REVOLUTIONARY MILITARY POLICY
T. DERBENT • 9781894946438

52 pp. • $5.00

An educational exploration of the concepts of military doctrine, strategy, tactics, operational art, bases of support, guerilla zones, liberated territories, and more. A study of what has been tried in the past, where different strategies worked, and where they failed, all from a perspective concerned with making revolution. (2013)

CHICAN@ POWER AND THE STRUGGLE FOR AZTLAN

CIPACTLI & EHECATL
9781894946742 • 320 pp. • $22.95

From the Amerikan invasion and theft of Mexican lands, to present day migrants risking their lives to cross the U.$. border, the Chican@ nation has developed in a cauldron of national oppression and liberation struggles. This book by a MIM(Prisons) Study Group presents the history of the Chican@ movement, exploring the colonialism and semi-colonialism that frames the Chican@ national identity. It also sheds new light on the modern repression and temptations that threaten liberation struggles by simultaneously pushing for submission and assimilation into Amerika. (2015)

THE COMMUNIST NECESSITY

J. MOUFAWAD-PAUL •
9781894946582 • 168 pp. • $10.00

A polemical interrogation of the practice of "social movementism" that has enjoyed a normative status at the centres of capitalism. Aware of his past affinity with social movementism, and with some apprehension of the problem of communist orthodoxy, the author argues that the recognition of communism's necessity "requires a new return to the revolutionary communist theories and experiences won from history." (2014)

CONFRONTING FASCISM: DISCUSSION DOCUMENTS FOR A MILITANT MOVEMENT
SECOND EDITION

XTN, D. HAMERQUIST, J.SAKAI,
M. SALOTTE • 9781894946872
219 pp. • $14.95

Understanding the relationship of fascism, the State, left reformism and what it means to be revolutionary are priorities in a world where it seems increasingly true that those who do not advance will have to retreat. Written in the early 2000s, from the perspective of revolutionaries active in the struggle against the far right. (2017)

CTRL-ALT-DELETE: AN ANTIFASCIST REPORT ON THE ALTERNATIVE RIGHT

MATTHEW N. LYONS,
ITS GOING DOWN, BROMMA
9781894946858 • 108 pp. • $10.00

An in-depth and timely look at the origins and rise of the so-called "alt-right," the fascistic movement that grabbed headlines in the months leading up to the 2016 election of Donald Trump as president of the United States. (2017)

DARING TO STRUGGLE, FAILING TO WIN: THE RED ARMY FACTION'S 1977 CAMPAIGN OF DESPERATION

ANDRÉ MONCOURT & J. SMITH
9781604860283 • 43 pp. • $4.00

A look at the Red Army Faction's activities in the seventies, and how their struggle to free their prisoners culminated in a campaign of assassinations and kidnappings in 1977. (2008)

DEFYING THE TOMB: SELECTED PRISON WRITINGS AND ART OF KEVIN "RASHID" JOHNSON FEATURING EXCHANGES WITH AN OUTLAW

KEVIN "RASHID" JOHNSON
9781894946391 • 386 pp. • $20.00

Follow the author's odyssey from lumpen drug dealer to prisoner, to revolutionary New Afrikan, a teacher and mentor, one of a new generation rising of prison intellectuals. (2010)

DIVIDED WORLD DIVIDED CLASS: GLOBAL POLITICAL ECONOMY AND THE STRATIFICATION OF LABOUR UNDER CAPITALISM
SECOND EDITION

ZAK COPE • 9781894946681
460 pp. • $24.95

Charting the history of the "labour aristocracy" in the capitalist world system, from its roots in colonialism to its birth and eventual maturation into a full-fledged middle class in the age of imperialism. Cope argues that pervasive national, racial and cultural chauvinism in the capitalist core represent the concentrated expressions of the major social strata of the core capitalist nations' shared economic interest in the exploitation and repression of dependent nations. (2015)

ESCAPING THE PRISM... FADE TO BLACK

JALIL MUNTAQIM • 9781894946629
320 pp. • $20.00

Poetry and essays from behind the bars of Attica prison. Combining the personal and the political, affording readers with a rare opportunity to get to know a man who has spent most of his life—over forty years—behind bars for his involvement in the Black Liberation Movement. Includes an extensive examination of the U.S. government's war against the Black Liberation Army in general, and Jalil in particular, by Ward Churchill, and an introduction by Walidah Imarisha. (2015)

EUROCENTRISM AND THE COMMUNIST MOVEMENT

ROBERT BIEL • 9781894946711
215 pp. • $17.95

Exploring the relationship between Eurocentrism, alienation, and racism, while tracing the different ideas about imperialism, colonialism, "progress," and non-European peoples as they were grappled with by revolutionaries in both the colonized and colonizing nations. Teasing out racist errors and anti-racist insights within this history, Biel reveals a century-long struggle to assert the centrality of the most exploited within the struggle against capitalism. (2015)

EXODUS AND RECONSTRUCTION: WORKING-CLASS WOMEN AT THE HEART OF GLOBALIZATION

BROMMA • 9781894946421
37 pp. • $3.00

The decline of traditional rural patriarchy and the position of women at the heart of a transformed global proletariat. (2013)

FIRE THE COPS: ESSAYS, LECTURES, AND JOURNALISM

KRISTIAN WILLIAMS, WITH PHOTOGRAPHS BY BETTE LEE
9781894946612 • 224 pp. • $20.00

Killer cops and cop-killers, "police as workers" and police as soldiers, copwatching and counterinsurgency operations … these subjects and more are examined in this collection of essays by veteran activist Kristian Williams. (2014)

THE HISTORICAL FAILURE OF ANARCHISM: IMPLICATIONS FOR THE FUTURE OF THE REVOLUTIONARY PROJECT

CHRISTOPHER DAY
9781894946452 • 26 pp. • $4.00

An exposition of the failure of anarchism to successfully carry out or defend revolution in the 20th century, raising questions for the future. (2009)

IS CHINA AN IMPERIALIST COUNTRY?

N.B. TURNER ET AL.
9781894946759 • 173 pp. • $17.00

Whether or not China is now a capitalist-imperialist country is an issue on which there is some considerable disagreement, even within the revolutionary left. This book brings together theoretical, definitional and logical considerations, as well as the extensive empirical evidence which is now available, to demonstrate that China has indeed definitely become a capitalist-imperialist country. (2015)

JAILBREAK OUT OF HISTORY: THE RE-BIOGRAPHY OF HARRIET TUBMAN & "THE EVIL OF FEMALE LOAFERISM"
SECOND EDITION

BUTCH LEE • 9781894946704
169 pp. • $14.95

Anticolonial struggles of New Afrikan/Black women were central to the unfolding of 19th century amerika, both during and "after" slavery. "The Re-Biography of Harriet Tubman" recounts the life and politics of Harriet Tubman, who waged and eventually lead the war against the capitalist slave system. "The Evil of Female Loaferism" details New Afrikan women's attempts to withdraw from and evade capitalist colonialism, an unofficial but massive labor strike which threw the capitalists North and South into a panic. The ruling class response consisted of the "Black Codes," Jim Crow, re-enslavement through prison labor, mass violence, and … the establishment of a neo-colonial Black patriarchy, whose task was to make New Afrikan women subordinate to New Afrikan men just as New Afrika was supposed to be subordinate to white amerika. (2015)

KARL MARX AND FRIEDRICH ENGELS: ON COLONIES, INDUSTRIAL MONOPOLY AND THE WORKING CLASS MOVEMENT

INTRODUCTION BY ZAK COPE & TORKIL LAUESEN • 9781894946797 160 pp. • $10.00

Excerpts from the corpus of Marx and Engels, showing the evolution of their ideas on the nascent labor aristocracy and the complicating factors of colonialism and chauvinism, with a focus on the British Empire of their time. In their introduction, Cope and Lauesen show how Marx and Engels's initial belief that capitalism would extend seamlessly around the globe in the same form was proven wrong by events, as instead worldwide imperialism spread capitalism as a polarizing process, not only between the bourgeoisie and the working class, but also as a division between an imperialist center and an exploited periphery. (2016)

LEARNING FROM AN UNIMPORTANT MINORITY

J. SAKAI 9781894946605 • 118 pp. • $10.00

Race is all around us, as one of the main structures of capitalist society. Yet, how we talk about it and even how we think about it is tightly policed. Everything about race is artificially distorted as a white/Black paradigm. Instead, we need to understand the imposed racial reality from many different angles of radical vision. In this talk given at the 2014 Montreal Anarchist Bookfair, J. Sakai shares experiences from his own life as a revolutionary in the united states, exploring what it means to belong to an "unimportant minority." (2015)

LUMPEN: THE AUTOBIOGRAPHY OF ED MEAD

ED MEAD • 9781894946780 360 pp. • $20.00

When a thirteen-year-old Ed Mead ends up in the Utah State Industrial School, a prison for boys, it is the first step in a story of oppression and revolt that will ultimately lead to the foundation of the George Jackson Brigade, a Seattle-based urban guerrilla group, and to Mead's re-incarceration as a fully engaged revolutionary, well-placed and prepared to take on both his captors and the predators amongst his fellow prisoners. This is his story. (2015)

MEDITATIONS ON FRANTZ FANON'S WRETCHED OF THE EARTH: NEW AFRIKAN REVOLUTIONARY WRITINGS

JAMES YAKI SAYLES 9781894946322 • 399 pp. • $20.00

One of those who eagerly picked up Fanon in the '60s, who carried out armed expropriations and violence against white settlers, Sayles reveals how behind the image of Fanon as race thinker there is an underlying reality of antiracist communist thought. (2010)

THE MILITARY STRATEGY OF WOMEN AND CHILDREN

BUTCH LEE • 0973143231 116 pp. • $12.00

Lays out the need for an autonomous and independent women's revolutionary movement, a revolutionary women's culture that involves not only separating oneself from patriarchal imperialism, but also in confronting, opposing, and waging war against it by all means necessary. (2003)

MY ENEMY'S ENEMY: ESSAYS ON GLOBALIZATION, FASCISM AND THE STRUGGLE AGAINST CAPITALISM

ANTI-FASCIST FORUM

0973143231 • 116 pp. • $10.00

Articles by anti-fascist researchers and political activists from Europe and North America, examining racist and pro-capitalist tendencies within the movement against globalization. (2003)

NIGHT-VISION: ILLUMINATING WAR & CLASS ON THE NEO-COLONIAL TERRAIN
SECOND EDITION

BUTCH LEE AND RED ROVER

9781894946889 • 280 pp. • $17.00

From *Night-Vision*: "The transformation to a neo-colonial world has only begun, but it promises to be as drastic, as disorienting a change as was the original european colonial conquest of the human race. Capitalism is again ripping apart & restructuring the world, and nothing will be the same. Not race, not nation, not gender, and certainly not whatever culture you used to have. Now you have outcast groups as diverse as the Aryan Nation and the Queer Nation and the Hip Hop Nation publicly rejecting the right of the u.s. government to rule them. All the building blocks of human culture—race, gender, nation, and especially class—are being transformed under great pressure to embody the spirit of this neo-colonial age." First published in 1998, *Night-Vision* provides the definitive analysis of postmodern capitalism, the decline of u.s. hegemony, and the need and possibilities for a revolutionary movement of the oppressed to overthrow it all. (2017)

OUR COMMITMENT IS TO OUR COMMUNITIES: MASS INCARCERATION, POLITICAL PRISONERS, AND BUILDING A MOVEMENT FOR COMMUNITY-BASED JUSTICE

DAVID GILBERT • 9781894946650

34 pp. • $5.00

Interviewed by Bob Feldman, political prisoner David Gilbert discusses the ongoing catastrophe that is mass incarceration, connecting it to the continued imprisonment of political prisoners and the challenges that face our movements today. (2014)

PANTHER VISION: ESSENTIAL PARTY WRITINGS AND ART OF KEVIN "RASHID" JOHNSON, MINISTER OF DEFENSE, NEW AFRIKAN BLACK PANTHER PARTY-PRISON CHAPTER

KEVIN "RASHID" JOHNSON

9781894946766 • 496 pp. • $24.95

The core writings from the Minister of Defense of the New Afrikan Black Panther Party–Prison Chapter. Subjects addressed include the differences between anarchism and Marxism-Leninsm, the legacy of the Black Panther Party, the timeliness of Huey P. Newton's concept of revolutionary intercommunalism, the science of dialectical and historical materialsm, the practice of democratic centralism, as well as current events ranging from u.s. imperialist designs in Africa to national oppression of New Afrikans within u.s. borders. (2015)

THE RED ARMY FACTION, A DOCUMENTARY HISTORY VOLUME 1: PROJECTILES FOR THE PEOPLE

ANDRÉ MONCOURT & J. SMITH EDS.
9781604860290 • 736 pp. • $34.95

The first in a three-volume series, by far the most in-depth political history of the Red Army Faction ever made available in English. This volume presents all of the manifestos and communiqués issued by the RAF between 1970 and 1977, along with the background to understand the context in which it all occurred. From Andreas Baader's prison break, through the 1972 May Offensive and the 1975 hostage-taking in Stockholm, to the desperate, and tragic, events of the "German Autumn" of 1977. The RAF's three main manifestos—The Urban Guerilla Concept, Serve the People, and Black September—are included, as are important interviews with *Spiegel* and *le Monde Diplomatique*, and a number of communiqués and court statements explaining their actions. (2009)

THE RED ARMY FACTION, A DOCUMENTARY HISTORY VOLUME 2: DANCING WITH IMPERIALISM

ANDRÉ MONCOURT & J. SMITH EDS.
9781604860306 • 480 pp. • $26.95

The second in a three-volume series, including the details of the guerilla's operations, and its communiqués and texts, from 1978 up until the 1984 offensive—a period of regrouping and reorientation for the RAF, with its previous focus on freeing its prisoners replaced by an anti-NATO orientation. With an introduction by Ward Churchill. (2013)

SETTLERS: THE MYTHOLOGY OF THE WHITE PROLETARIAT FROM MAYFLOWER TO MODERN

J. SAKAI • 9781629630373
456 pp. • $20.00

Am sobering appraisal of America's white citizenry, showing that they have never supported themselves but have always resorted to exploitation and theft, culminating in acts of genocide to maintain their culture and way of life. As recounted in painful detail by Sakai, the United States has been built on the theft of Indigenous lands and of Afrikan labor, on the robbery of the northern third of Mexico, the colonization of Puerto Rico, and the expropriation of the Asian working class, with each of these crimes being accompanied by violence. This new edition includes "Cash & Genocide: The True Story of Japanese-American Reparations" and an interview with the author by Ernesto Aguilar. (2014)

STAND UP STRUGGLE FORWARD: NEW AFRIKAN REVOLUTIONARY WRITINGS ON NATION, CLASS AND PATRIARCHY

SANYIKA SHAKUR
9781894946469 • 208 pp. • $13.95

This collection of writings by Sanyika Shakur, formerly known as Monster Kody Scott, includes several essays written from within the infamous Pelican Bay Security Housing Unit in the period around the historic 2011 California prisoners' hunger strike, as well as two interviews conducted just before and after his release in Black August 2012. Shakur rejects the easy answers and false solutions of the neocolonial age—integration and racism, the colonial-criminal mentality